DISCOVERING THE SMALLEST CHURCHES IN ENGLAND

DISCOVERING THE SMALLEST CHURCHES IN ENGLAND

JOHN KINROSS

To all fellow Readers

First published 2003 by Weidenfeld & Nicolson
This edition first published 2008
Reprinted 2015

The History Press Ltd
The Mill, Brimscombe Port
Stroud, Gloucestershire, GL5 2QG
www.thehistorypress.co.uk

© John Kinross 2003, 2008

The right of John Kinross to be identified as the Author of this work has been asserted in accordance with the Copyrights, Designs and Patents Act 1988.

All rights reserved. No part of this book may be reprinted or reproduced or utilised in any form or by any electronic, mechanical or other means, now known or hereafter invented, including photocopying and recording, or in any information storage or retrieval system, without the permission in writing from the Publishers.

British Library Cataloguing in Publication Data.
A catalogue record for this book is available from the British Library.

ISBN 978 0 7524 4779 7

Typesetting and origination by The History Press Ltd.
Printed in Great Britain

CONTENTS

List of Illustrations	7
Foreword & Acknowledgements	8
Introduction	9
Bedfordshire	11
Berkshire	14
Buckinghamshire	17
Cambridgeshire	21
Channel Islands	25
Cheshire	27
Cornwall	29
Cumberland	32
Derbyshire	34
Devon	36
Dorset	40
Durham	45
Essex	47
Gloucestershire	50
Hampshire	56
Herefordshire	60
Hertfordshire	62
Huntingdonshire	65
Isle of Man	67
Isle of Wight	69
Kent	71
Lancashire	75
Leicestershire	78
Lincolnshire	81
London	84
London's Smallest Church	87

Middlesex	89
Norfolk	91
Northamptonshire	94
Northumberland	96
Nottinghamshire	99
Oxfordshire	101
Rutland	105
Shropshire	107
Somerset	110
Staffordshire	114
Suffolk	116
Surrey	120
Sussex (East)	123
Sussex (West)	125
Warwickshire	128
Westmorland	130
Wiltshire	131
Worcestershire	136
Yorkshire (East)	138
Yorkshire (North)	141
Yorkshire (West)	143
Glossary	146
Bibliography	149
Appendix I	151
Appendix II	151
Appendix III	152
Index of Churches by Place Name	156
General Index	158

LIST OF ILLUSTRATIONS

Monochrome Figures

All Saints, Fleet Marston 18
Fitzwilliam Chapel, Cambridge 23
St John, Bodinnic 31
St Edwold, Stockwood 41
St Cuthbert, Oborne 42
St Nicholas, Arne 43
All Saints, Wrabness 48
St Michael, Duntisbourne Rous 51
Door Handle at Syde 52
Bellcote at Farmcote 53
All Saints, Radwell 63
St Lawrence Old Church,
 Isle of Wright 70
St James, Sutton Cheney 79
St Pancras, London 87
All Saints, Shorthampton 103
St Beuno, Culbone 111
Swell font and church 112
All Saints, Sutton Bingham 113
King Charles the Martyr, Shelland 117
St Mary, Thornton Parva 118
St Mary, North Marden 125
St James, Buttermere 132
St Laurence, Bradford-on-Avon 133
St Peter, Blackland 134
Speeton, Stone cross & Agnus Dei 139

Colour Plates
(between pages 96 & 97)

1 St Michael, Farndish
2 St Thomas, East Shefford
3 All Saints, Little Kimble
4 Guyhirn, Cambridgeshire
5 Our Lady & St Anne, Widemouth Bay
6 St Edith, Shocklach
7 St Mary, Honeychurch
8 St Bega, Bassenthwaite
9 St Martin, Wareham
10 St Michael de Rupe, Brentor
11 St Peter's Chapel, Bradwell-Juxta-Mare
12 St John, Elkstone
13 St Mary, Syde
14 St Hubert, Idsworth
15 Fresco at St Hubert, Idsworth
16 St John, Little Gidding
17 St Margaret, St Margarets
18 Sixteenth-century screen at
 St Margaret
19 St Margaret, Waddingworth
20 St Lawrence, Cowley
21 Chapel of St John,
 The Tower of London
22 All Saints, Keswick, Norfolk
23 St Andrew, Sookholme
24 St Giles, Carburton
25 St Oswald, Widford
26 St Beuno, Culbone
27 St Peter, Melverley
28 St Peter, Melverley - interior
29 Langley Chapel, Shropshire - interior
30 St Michael, Up Marden
31 Church of the Good Shepherd,
 Lullington
32 St Michael, Hanley Childe
33 Kempe Window at St Leonard,
 Chapel-le-Dale

FOREWORD & ACKNOWLEDGEMENTS

The parish churches of England are one of the glories of our country. One could make a reasonable claim that they have been better preserved and maintained during the past one hundred years than ever before in their history. That this is so is in large measure due to the efforts of local communities and a series of regular inspections by the diocesan authorities. Churches, like friendships, need to be kept in constant repair.

John Kinross in this book introduces us to some of England's smallest churches. Many are well-cared for, not a few have been rescued and restored – they are obviously cherished by those who frequent them. Others, alas, in thinly populated areas, are less fortunate and visitors will share his hope that more might be done and better days lie ahead. His love for these small buildings springs from his experience that in visiting churches 'it is the small, musty ones that seemed to speak to us more of God'. Often in remote spots, the search is rewarding: 'once inside … there is peace, wonder, quiet'.

The author's sense of history, his knowledge of architecture, the pertinacity in the quest 'oe'r moor and fen, o'er crag and torrent', and his whimsical sense of humour make him an engaging companion as well as a reliable guide. Readers will enjoy his economical descriptions of the churches, and the pleasing illustrations whet one's appetite to join him on his journeys. Here are buildings that stir the imagination, and move us to think about the people who built them, those who have worshipped in them down the centuries, the sounds of their voices and the variety of their petitions in peace time and war, in sorrow and anxiety, thanksgiving and celebration. They incite us to come alongside them – 'to kneel where prayer has been valid'.

– Rt Revd Colin James
Former Bishop of Winchester

The author owes his thanks to Canon Anthony Johnson for all his help, to Revd Stephen Cope, Canon Peter Lawrence and other members of the Rural Theology Association, to the Lincolnshire Old Churches Trust, the Round Tower Churches Society, the Romney Marsh Historical Churches Trust and, especially, Mrs Poole of the Churches Conservation Trust. In Kent I was guided by John Vigar and Hon. Henry Maude and, on the trek to see St Lawrence Bradwell-Juxta-Mare, by the late Tony Teague. In Shropshire my guide was Bernard Lowry, in Hertfordshire Jane Kelsall, in Surrey and Hampshire, John Stevenson and in the Isle of Man, James and Helen Stevenson. Also, I would like to give a special thanks to all Diocesan Secretaries who have sent me lists of their smallest churches. A special thanks goes to John Taylor for the maps and also to Rt Revd Colin James, former Bishop of Winchester, for writing the Foreword.

INTRODUCTION

Another book on churches, you may well ask? Is there a need for it? For many years a friend of mine has accompanied me round churches in the South West. Early on in our tours I realised that it was the small, musty ones that seemed to speak to us more of God. They may be difficult to find, the path to them may lead across a boggy field, the door sometimes needs a rugby footballer's heave to open it, but once inside it is a different matter. There is peace, wonder, quiet; all elements sadly missing in our world today.

There is a useful saying: 'Saxons Never Eat Danish Pies' which is helpful in remembering the styles of church architecture:

Saxon	up to 1066
Norman	1066–1200
Early English	1200–1300
Decorated	1250–1350
Perpendicular	1350–1530

Thus in Saxon times we get the aisle-less church, as at Escomb, Durham. In Norman times there are more often carved doorways and chancel arches as at Barfreston, Kent. Early English work can be seen at Arne, Dorset and Perpendicular churches are common in the Cotswolds – the famous wool churches of Cirencester and Chipping Camden, for example. Sometimes there are Tudor windows or other decorations as at Farmcote, Gloucestershire. Then there are some churches in a style all of their own, like Willen, Bucks, a 1670 'town' church transferred to the countryside.

Sometimes it is a good idea to make a drawing of the floor plan of the church you are visiting, adding the windows, font, pulpit and other outstanding points. If you are short of time, then buy a guide book and put the points in when you get home. A friend can help. He or she may concentrate on the windows and you can compare notes later. In this way you will remember the churches you visit.

In this book I have tried to include other churches to see nearby, what to do if the church is locked – there is often a key-holder very close, or a line to the vicar before you go can be helpful. Our guide last summer took us round about 25 different churches in a week. Only one was locked. It was in the process of an Interregnum so there was no single person in charge. The Churches Conservation Trust publish little county guides with opening details in them. Lincolnshire and Norfolk have guide books and flourishing societies that can help. In the back of this book there is a useful list of addresses.

The Revd Gordon Gatward, now at Stoneleigh Agricultural Centre, was one of the main speakers at the Rural Theology Conference at Salisbury Theological College in 1995. The theme was 'The Holy Place' and some of those present expected a lecture on churches. However, we didn't get this. Instead Gordon explored areas that are regarded as 'holy' due to an event or action. He pointed out that today, when someone is killed in a roadside accident, the relatives often put flowers beside the road. For example in Cornwall, there is a small garden by the main road just outside Truro. To the affected family, the spot is sacred; a holy place indeed.

Gordon's words rang true. For the first nine years of my life I was at boarding school. Those of you in similar positions will remember the small bed space. You were lucky to have a locker and if you got out of bed, literally, on the wrong side, you were trespassing onto someone else's space. Later in the forces it was worse than this. We were very cramped and space had to be found for uniform. Lockers were not allowed to have pin-ups and privacy was almost non-existent. Overseas some of us lived in a converted stable in Aden. There were shutters, no glass in the windows, no carpets, a flat roof that leaked when it rained (a rare event), but a balcony overlooking the Red Sea. We lived in this building for nearly two years and personally I never got used to so little bed space. What I did have became holy. Thus was born my love of small 'holy' spaces. There needs to be enough space to pray, to stand and to not feel closed in like poor Lord Lovel of Minster Lovell, who shut himself up in a secret room with his bible after the Battle of Stoke. Many years later his skeleton was discovered by builders knocking down a wall.

During the Gunpowder Plot, many Catholics had secret priest holes, where their priests could hide until they could safely take a service. Such a place, Boscobel House, was later used to good effect by the escaping Charles II. Today we have a Roman Catholic chapel at Keele University, which was never designed as a holy place, but opens up to reveal its altar at the touch of a button. I have included this in my book because it is such a surprise for those of us brought up in the middle-of-the-road Church of England.

Where do we go next? I have included one other University Chapel in this book and recommend it as an architectural masterpiece of the twentieth century. This is the college chapel of Fitzwilliam College, Cambridge. You have to make an effort to find it, like so many of the churches in this book, but when you do it is well worthwhile. There is a message here perhaps and all the churches chosen are a personal choice. There are a few chapels – as in Guernsey and Jersey – included as they are eminently worth seeing and not necessarily on the tourist route. I have accepted the Friar definition of a church as 'A building used for public Christian worship', adding the word 'consecrated', and of chapels as 'from $c.$800 sacred buildings less [important] than churches.' What then constitutes a 'small church' you may well ask? I have used the dimension of a 30ft nave or less and seating for 50 people or less. I have omitted all ruins and prefer churches that are used at least once a year to those permanently closed.

BEDFORDSHIRE

Our four small churches are very different from each other. The north of the county has many stone buildings like neighbouring Northamptonshire. The south is more akin to Buckinghamshire. I have chosen churches from each.

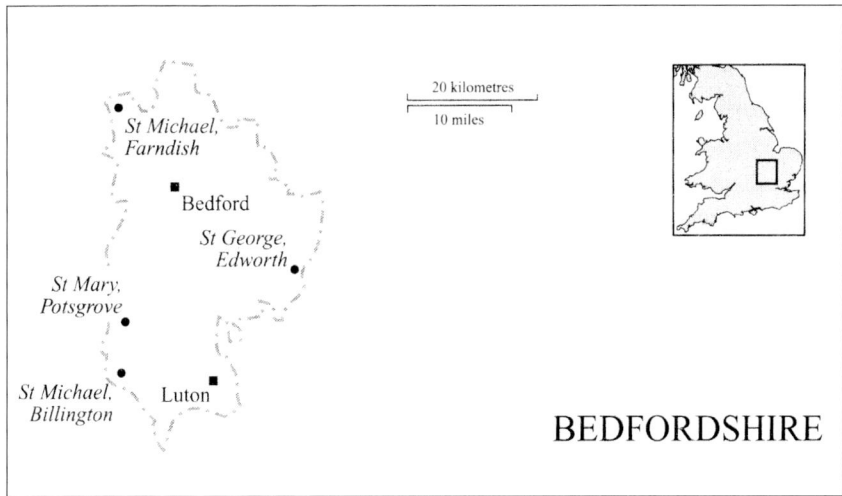

St Michael, Farndish

This must be the smallest church in the county and Farndish is not an easy hamlet to find. It lies 4 miles south-east of Wellingborough off the B569 and is signposted from Irthington. The key is obtainable from the farm called Aldermans and many of the Alderman family have tombs in the church. Originally twelfth century with a low fifteenth-century tower, the church is in the hands of the Churches Conservation Trust and is in need of friends. Outside, there are some interesting corbels, but the gem is the Norman font and its seventeenth-century cover which has 'One Lord, One Father, One Baptism, One God and Father of all who is above all' written around the base. The nave is 30ft in length and someone had put hymns 34 and 218 on the board so there must have been a service fairly recently.

The tower was constructed inside the nave in the fifteenth century. The Early English south doorway has three orders of shafts, but only two are attached. The shafts are made of orange ironstone, which alternates with grey limestone. The box pews have Victorian panelling. This is a church worth discovering.

St Michael & All Angels, Billington. *Courtesy of B. Pollard*

St Michael & All Angels, Billington

A few miles from Leighton Buzzard, Billington Church is on top of a hill, which has long been an ancient watch post. There may also have been a pagan shrine. The original church was a chapel of ease with a square wooden bell tower.

There is a thirteenth-century blank window inside the west wall that looks as if it has been re-set. The vestry on the west side looks as if the Friar Tucks of this world would have had to enter backwards as there would not be much space to turn round when fully robed!

In 1869, Billington became a parish and, although Victorianised, the nave and chancel are basically thirteenth century. The bell tower was replaced by a Victorian spire from nearby St Barnabas, Linslade. Much of the glass is from the workshop of Mayer of Munich. There is a small brass plaque to commemorate Arthur Murgett who died in 'Japanese hands' in 1943 aged 22 and another to Cuthbert Pratt who died in the First World War aged only 19. They would be proud of the care and use that goes into St Michaels. On the way out, children will be pleased to see the carpenter's small mouse on the lich gate.

Other churches to see in Bedfordshire:

St George, Edworth

Once part of St Neot's Priory, Edworth is on the Hertfordshire border. Built about 1200, it has Decorated two-bay aisles and a west tower. The crenellation, clerestory and two porches are Decorated. The benches have ogee ends, one carved with a monkey, one a lion and one a monster. The church is also in the care of the Churches Conservation Trust with a key-holder nearby. It is 3 miles south-east of Biggleswade.

St Mary, Potsgrove

Potsgrove is in farming country south of Woburn. This is a fourteenth-century church rebuilt in 1880 by J.D. Sedding, who was involved in the Arts and Crafts movement. There is a fourteenth-century restored screen and brasses to Richard Saunders and his wife (1535) and to William Saunders (1563) on a palimpsest brass. The church is cared for by the Churches Conservation Trust and the key is kept nearby.

BERKSHIRE

Berkshire, the Royal county, is now slug-shaped, having lost some of its land to Oxfordshire in the 1970s. The glories of Windsor Chapel are at one end and certainly should not be missed, but the two smallest churches are both close together in the 'down' end of the county where racehorses are a common sight.

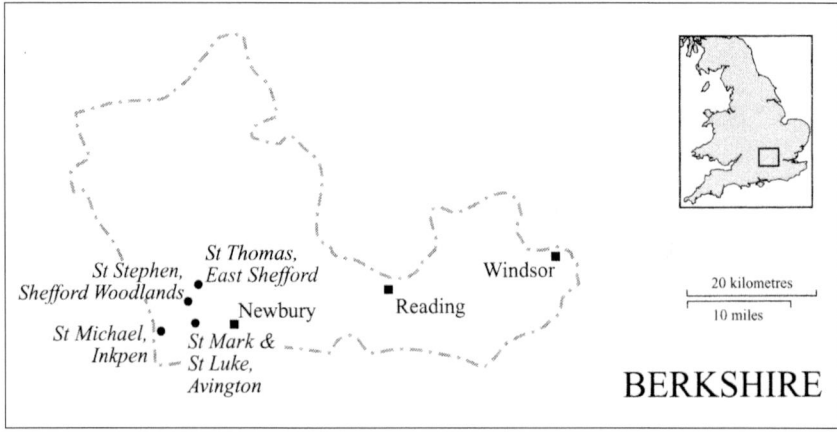

St Stephen, Shefford Woodlands

A former Wesleyan chapel, St Stephen's does not appear in Pevsner's *Berkshire,* but neither does the village and thus it is easy to miss. Close to the M4, it is just off the Hungerford turning. On the road to Wantage take the second right and then right again. Outside, the rendered building looks dull and of no interest, but inside it is a memorial to the villagers who died in the Great War. The chapel fell into disuse at the end of the nineteenth century and a woodcarver, Captain Burmester, proposed to the Oxfordshire Registry that it become a Church of England church. The Bishop of Oxford dedicated it on Shrove Tuesday, 1911. Captain Burmester turned it into a memorial church after 11 men from the village lost their lives in the First World War. All have their names engraved on the backs of the pews and the south windows have pictures of war and peace, the latter showing the village and including the church in 1920. Opposite is the house *Lovelocks,* home of General Godley and another window is in memory of Alicia, his wife and organist who died in 1946. Today, Shefford Woodlands is well looked-after and there is a monthly service, the main church for the community being Great Shefford.

St Thomas, East Shefford

The second smallest church is no distance away and is in the hands of the Churches Conservation Trust. A few miles along the road is Great Shefford. Turn left just after the sign and you come to East Shefford, a hamlet with a large farm. Go through the gates, over a bridge and then park by the hedge. The little church is 100 yards along a path. The key is in a box by the metal gate. The original building was the Fettiplace Manor chapel. Thomas Fettiplace married Beatrice, a member of the Portuguese Royal Family. Their tomb – she died in 1447 – is in the church and you fall into it when you enter via the little door. Note the yellow-glazed floor tiles, whitewashed walls and remains of wall paintings. The stone coffin lid comes from a coffin found in 1873 near the south door. In it was a priest clutching a pewter chalice and paten. Harold Victor Armstrong, personally responsible for saving St Thomas's, has his own 1979 monument on the wall. There are also two brasses on the north wall, presumably Fettiplaces. The nave is 28ft 10in and in it is a stack of chairs which indicates that there is an occasional service.

A new church was built, but was later demolished according to Pevsner (1966), and the old church was saved by Friends of the Friendless Churches and the Churches Conservation Trust.

There are wall paintings on the chancel arch. The Ten Commandments appear on the north wall and different texts appear in other places, so they probably date from different times. There is a 1480 helmet, known as a salade, in the sanctuary which belonged to one of the Fettiplace family. Presumably when he put it on it gave a whole new meaning to the phrase 'Salade Dressing'.

This is a lonely church in a wonderful setting. Perhaps one day it will be used again.

Other churches to see in Berkshire:

St Mark & St Luke, Avington

Not far from the two Sheffords, Avington Church is on Avington Park estate and looked after by the Churches Conservation Trust. The key is on a hook by the cottage door of one of the cottages you pass on the way down to the church.

It is a Norman building with zigzag moulding on south door and chancel arch. The Norman font has carvings of a bishop, man, devil, two devils and an atlas in Italian style. It is most unusual. There are strange beakheads on the chancel pillars and it is thought the chancel was never finished as intended.

Outside there is a huge cedar tree and the estate workers use the church on occasions.

St Michael, Inkpen

Close to the Berkshire–Wiltshire border below Hungerford, Inkpen is a nave-and-chancel-in-one church. The doorway is thirteenth century, but most of the church was restored by C.C. Rolfe in 1896. There is an Arts & Crafts south window. The nave was widened at some time, as the timber posts of the bell turret stand free. There is a battered knight effigy, unknown, and some memorial bible pictures on the walls put there by the Butlers of Inkpen.

BUCKINGHAMSHIRE

There is a diversification of churches in this county – some fairly unknown – and as far as groups go, the Aylesbury fonts of the late twelfth century are seen at Aylesbury, Great Kimble, Chenies, the Missendens, Wing and Bledlow. The Ivinghoe thirteenth-century carved capitals can be seen at Pitstone, Eaton Bray (Bedfordshire) and Flamstead (Hertfordshire) as well. However, the three smallest churches are very different. Two are hidden in the roundabouts of Milton Keynes and even with a map are not easy to track down. The other, All Saints, Little Kimble, is quite easy.

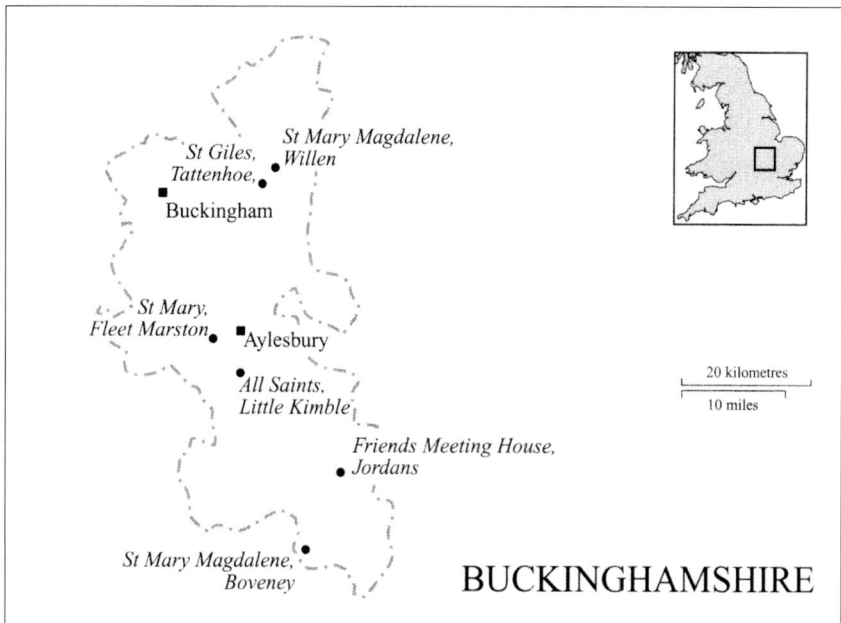

All Saints, Little Kimble

This stands close up on a road junction just off the A4100, under the delightful Cymbeline's mount. The neighbouring church, Ellesborough, is used by the visiting prime ministers and their families when at Chequers. Little Kimble is famous for its wall paintings, the best in the county. All the walls were covered with paintings of saints at one time, with the west wall reserved for a Doom painting or Last Judgement scene. The 11 saints still recognizable are St Lawrence,

St Francis preaching to his birds, St Clare, St George and a princess, St Christopher, St James the Great, St Margaret (scenes from her life) St Bernard and St Catherine of Alexandria. The paintings have to be kept at an even temperature to stop them disintegrating.

None are in very good shape and personally I would like to see them all restored. Pictures of them and details are given in E. Clive Rouse's excellent *Medieval Wall Paintings* (Shire, rp. 1996). Don't forget to see the Chertsey tiles by the altar decorated with scenes of King Mark of Cornwall.

Apart from its wall paintings, Little Kimble Church is where John Hampden made his famous protest against Ship Money, a protest that led, with other causes, to the Civil War.

St Mary, Fleet Marston

On the other side of Aylesbury just off the A41, the small church here is easy to miss. Stop at the Hunter Garden Centre to borrow the key (to the priest's door not the main one) and the footpath goes through the reclamation yard. Here was a lost village and the church has only survived due to the Churches Conservation Trust.

The nave, chancel and font date from the twelfth century, the chancel arch was rebuilt in the fourteenth century and the strong roof, with queen-posts, dates from the fifteenth century. No one knew just how good a roof it was until 1868, when Scott removed the plaster ceiling. In the 1960s the church was frequently vandalised. The man living in the Old Rectory next door looked out one day to see two men

All Saints, Fleet Marston, Buckinghamshire © *Author*

carrying off the altar table. With the help of Mr Hunter, the landowner, they were persuaded to put it back and the locks had to be changed. His daughter was later married in the church, so it is used on special occasions. St Mary is also famous as one of the first churches John Wesley preached in after his ordination.

St Giles, Tattenhoe

This is the smallest church in the county and probably the most difficult to find. Take the A421 to Milton Keynes and turn down Road VI where there is a sign saying Tattenhoe Park and, opposite this, a lane leading to various building sites. At the end of this is a car park and an expanse of green grass. Amidst the yew trees is a tiny church and a pond belonging to the long-vanished mansion. There was a chapel here that was converted in 1540 into a small church built from the stones of Snelshall Priory. The interior has box pews, pulpit, altar rails and floor dating to about 1800. The Christmas service in candlelight we attended in 2002 was a great success – some 40 attended – and it seems the Vicar comes from some miles away. It is kept firmly locked.

Inside, St Giles suffers from damp, which is a nightmare for cash-struck church wardens and Parish Church Councils. There are painted box pews and high-backed pews, mostly Victorian, and a seventeenth-century oak altar table and nineteenth-century font. All windows have had to be protected by polycarbonate due to air rifle vandals, hence the locks. The nave and chancel together measure 40ft x 13ft 6in. The new buildings of Milton Keynes are rapidly encroaching on St Giles. Let us hope there will soon be a few more supporters of this tiny building living nearby.

St Mary Magdalene, Willen

At the other corner of Milton Keynes and a bit easier to find is Willen and in the park on the edge of the lake close to the M1 is a London City church built in the countryside. Robert Hooke, a contemporary of Wren, was the architect and the funds came from Dr Busby, headmaster of Westminster School, whose portrait hangs inside. St Mary is brick built and the windows have been replaced by metal ones – quite successfully – but inside the décor is all 1680.

Entering St Mary is almost breath-taking. Here is a wonderful 1680 Caroline interior. There is a tunnel-vaulted ceiling. The décor is a shade of pink, the pews all have candle holders. There is a hexagonal pulpit and the font has a black polygonal baluster and is made of white marble. The font cover, ogee-shaped, has an urn on top with carved flowers, fruit and cherubs round the base. It is by Baines, who carved font covers for Wren.

Of the two rooms to the left and right of the doorway, one used to be Dr Busby's library, the other a vestry. They were locked so I couldn't check on this. The tower, with its pineapple finials, has two curved-top windows imitating the door and a circular window in the middle. That Buckinghamshire, always a Parliamentary county with its Hampden associations, should sing such a song after the Restoration is something we have to thank Dr Busby and his architect Robert Hooke for, and it is not their fault that Willen has become part of the sprawl of Milton Keynes.

Other churches to see in Buckinghamshire:

St Mary Magdalene, Boveney

Close to the River Thames between Eton and Dornay, St Mary was a ruin. Restored by the Friends of Friendless Churches, it now has a brick plinth round it. Built of flint and chalk it is a simple building once used by bargees and river folk. To get to it there is a footpath from Old Place.

Friends Meeting House, Jordans

Not far from Penn is this 1688 Quaker Meeting House built by Isaac Pennington. There is a caretaker's home inside which in 1773 was connected to the main meeting room by shutters. There is a small picture on the wall, sent from the USA, of a Red Indian raid on an American meeting house, with bonneted ladies carrying on with their service and ignoring the terrifying noises outside. In the graveyard is buried William Penn, founder of Pennsylvania (d.1718). The farm next door is a Quaker hostel and the barn is supposed to have been built out of timber from *The Mayflower*.

The Meeting House was badly damaged by fire, but has since been restored.

CAMBRIDGESHIRE

The county is like Essex and Hertfordshire in the south, but in the north there is fen country in the Isle of Ely. The cathedral of Ely stands like a great bull in a large field still dominating the landscape. The first church of small stature is St Mary, Mepal.

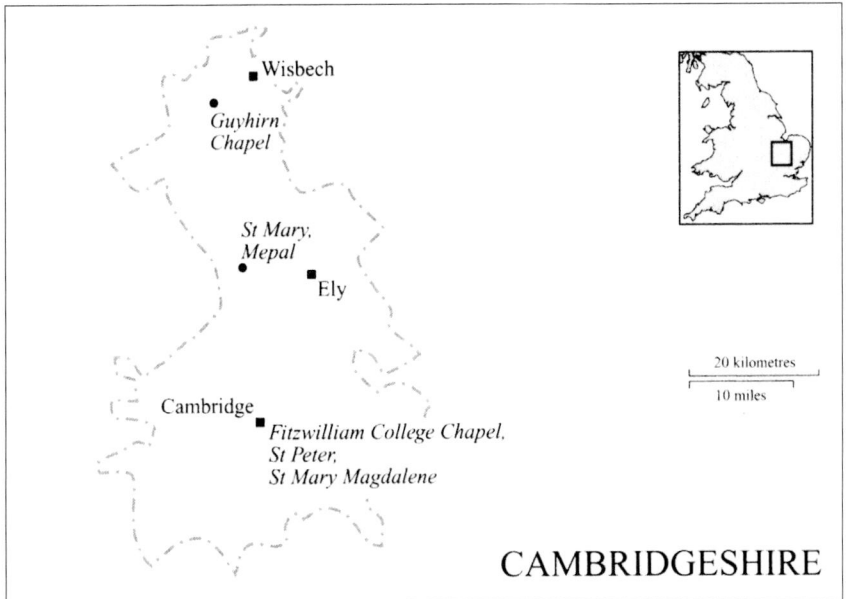

St Mary, Mepal

A few miles north of Ely on a fen, Mepal village church is visible in the middle of a field and some ancient oak trees. To reach it take Bridge Road – the bridge leads nowhere. Stop at the 'Three Peverells' and collect the key from Grove House near the pub. The footpath goes via the pub garden for the 200 yards to the church.

This small church has been much restored in 1849, 1876 and again by Caröe in 1905. It comes under Ely Diocese, seats about 40 and seems to be lovingly looked after. It is an Early English church with a steep roof and lancet windows in the chancel. There is an interesting memorial to James Fortra, a native of Brabant, who became Groom to the Bedchamber of Queen Mary of Modena. He did not escape to the continent with her and James II in 1688, but remained in obscurity in Mepal until his death aged 63. Like the monument in St James, Sutton Cheney (see p.79) this is an example of loyalty – a rather forgotten virtue today.

Fitzwilliam College Chapel

One of the newest Cambridge chapels, and only completed in 1995, it is in the middle of Lasdun's courtyard buildings and is found on the first floor. It is enclosed in a round brick tower. The visitor is taken by surprise as it opens up from the top of stairs. In fact, the space seems larger than it is (barely 40ft from organ to the boat-shaped altar). The east window has plain glass with the metalwork making a cross. The chairs are grouped in a semi-circle, but can be rearranged for concerts. The high ceiling, lighting and atmosphere make this a living chapel unlike many others. The only thing that spoils it is the grand piano tucked away beside the organ. The college has a full-time chaplain so the chapel is used all the year round.

The architect, Sir Richard MacCormac, writes:

> The place of worship is a vessel – an ark – held up and enclosed within two great cusps. The ark represents the idea of passage and protection, an archaic metaphor which recurs at conscious and unconscious levels – the 'nave' of a church, the 'night sea-journey' of myth and of religious and human experience – Jonah and the Whale, Noah's Ark, the womb, the cradle and the coffin. In the Christian symbolism of medieval manuscripts, the ship signifies the way of salvation. More literally the scheme draws on the Oslo Viking Ship Museum and the Vasa Ship Museum in Stockholm, where wooden vessels are contained and sheltered by buildings. The building itself is a combination of orthogonal structure, and a round enclosure. The plan can be read as a cross, projecting from the residential building, clasped by two arcs. The cruciform is embodied in the raised floor of the Chapel which is supported by four pairs of columns which in turn support the roof. The two main rooms, the meeting room and the Chapel itself have been placed one above the other. This gives the Chapel an appropriate scale in relation to the three-storey residential buildings. But more important is the sense that the meeting room is like a crypt, a kind of underworld, above which the important place – the Chapel itself – is raised.
>
> The Chapel itself can seat 36 people in a group without feeling too large and up to 136 people in a conventional aisled arrangement. It can be entered directly from the cloister, but latecomers have their own access and the chaplain has her own stair from below. This stair might also be used for dramatic or musical occasions. The meeting room can seat up to 46 people.
>
> *The New Chapel: Architect's Description*, Sir Richard MacCormac

There are three small churches, two of which are redundant, which are worth seeing in Cambridgeshire. First is St Peter's, Cambridge, near Magdalene Bridge, which is in the care of the Churches Conservation Trust. This little church in Castle Street is

Fitzwilliam Chapel, Cambridge © *Author*

originally of the eleventh century, but was later given a tower and spire. The original nave and chancel were demolished in 1791 and replaced with the present one-cell building. The most interesting item inside is the font, carved with two mermen clutching their tails. (The key for this church is at the Kettle's Yard Art Gallery.)

Secondly, near Barnwell Station (key from Station House), is the **Old Leper Chapel, St Mary Magdalene**, Newmarket Road which is a simple two-cell church with Norman zigzag moulding, the church set well below road level. There is a Friends of the Leper Chapel Group that looks after this building which is part of Holy Cross Parish and is still used for services. Treatment of lepers ceased in the nearby hospital in 1279, but the chapel did not cease to be used until 1751 and became a store, used in the local fair. In 1836 it was purchased by Thomas Kerridge who presented it to the university. Hence it made its way to the Cambridge Preservation Society. Services are held at 9am on the first Sunday of the month and 6.30pm on the fourth Sunday. David Bellamy is a Patron and the Bishop of Ely a Vice-Patron.

Of greater interest, though just too long for a small church, is **Guyhirn Chapel**, a seventeenth-century non-conformist chapel, situated in a graveyard but used as a chapel of ease, and repaired by the local Vicar. The seating is close together – benches with backs and no space for kneeling – and there is no altar, only a lectern. Guyhirn has the date 1660 on the door, but the money for its building was left by a wealthy Puritan in 1651 when Cromwell was in power. The simple four-light windows of plain glass, brick walls and floors are all in the Puritan mould so the date seems out of place. If you visit it (key from Post Office) don't forget to call in at March St Wendreda just to see the famous double hammerbeam angel roof. March is about half an hour's drive from Mepal on the A142 to Chatteris, then the A141 to Guyhirn. Normally I would not have stopped at such a large church, but there were two good reasons – the angels and more practically it was lunchtime and to find the key to St Wendreda you have to call at the local inn.

CHANNEL ISLANDS

A very special part of the world, the Channel Isles are individualistic. Jersey is more French, more independent perhaps than Guernsey, which is very English. Both have small chapels that are only just on the tourist map and worth visiting. They could scarcely be more different. Most of the Guernsey children were evacuated during the last war whereas most of the Jersey youngsters remained at home with their parents. The two islands do not mix much, but tourists can fly easily between the two without trouble or catch the hydrofoil that goes between the two main islands and Sark. Both islands have useful bus services and car hire is simple.

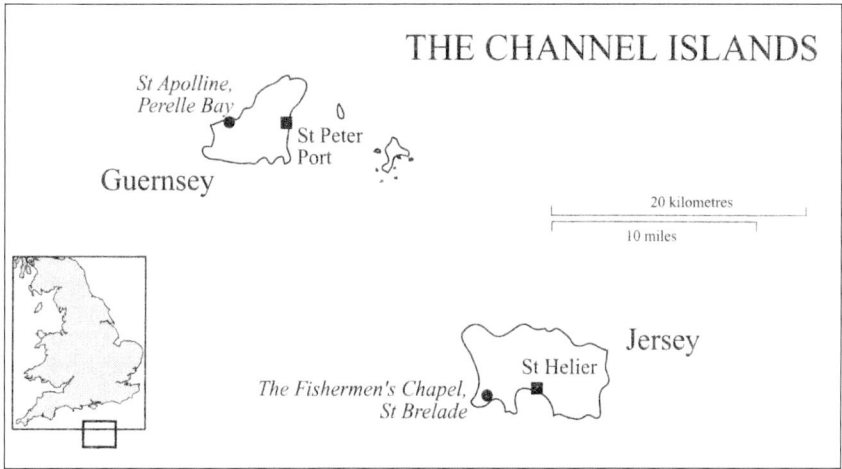

Guernsey

The chapel of St Apolline is in the Route de la Perelle and stands by itself next to the road. Slightly smaller than the Fishermen's Chapel on Jersey, it was completely restored in the 1970s and is used for ecumenical services. Who was St Apolline? She is the patron saint of dentists and was martyred about AD 250 when she was a deaconess in Alexandria. The Romans removed her teeth and then prepared a fire to burn her, giving her the option of praying to Roman gods or of being burnt alive. This was no problem to Apolline and she jumped into the fire.

The chapel was built about 1394 when it is mentioned in a charter of King Richard II as 'La Chapelle de St Marie de Perelle'. The builder, Nicholas Henry, paid for a chaplain to celebrate divine service every day and pray for the souls of himself and his wife Philippe. In 1873 it was purchased in a run-down state by the States of Guernsey and is now restored with a Cotswold stone roof, stone floor, Purbeck marble altar and new pews. There is a simple round stone above the altar with a cross cut into it and the stained glass window above the cross fits in well with its surroundings. The only jarring item is the chandelier and it is hoped that the wall painting of the last supper will be restored in time. The photographer has to be quick as the lights are on a time switch. The feast of St Apolline is on the 9 February and, according to the notice outside the building, there are services 'from time to time' for Christian Unity. The whole building and garden are beautifully looked after.

There is documentary evidence of the foundation in 1392 by Nicholas Henry who obtained a licence to erect a chapel on the manor he held of the abbey at Perelle. The chaplain had to swear fealty to the Prior of Vale and in 1394 the licence was confirmed by letters patent of King Richard III.

The chapel is 25ft long, 12ft wide and the walls are 8ft high. Although not a parish church, it certainly ranks as one of the smallest places of worship I have seen.

Jersey

The smallest church in Jersey stands next to St Brelade's church on the coast opposite St Helier. It is known as The Fishermen's Chapel. From outside the chapel is a rectangular building of uncertain age with two small crosses at the east and west ends. It looks like an armoury or a carpenter's shop, both of which it has been, and originally the site was occupied by a simple monastic church. The Reformation did away with such places and in 1550 the chapel became an armoury. For 400 years it had a large opening in the west wall for cannon to be drawn in and out for coastal defence.

In 1883, after a brief period as a carpenter's shop and store, it became a meeting room. The wall paintings were restored in 1918 and are very fine. They depict Adam and Eve, the fall of man, the Annunciation, the life of Christ and the Crucifixion, and they date from 1375 and 1425. The whole chapel was restored in the 1970s by Revd Michael Halliwell. There is a simplicity about the interior, with its six chairs made by Alan Peters, wall benches and granite floor made from irregular sized and different coloured stones. The lighting is from discreet wall lights and two modern standard lights. The whole effect is very pleasing and yet there is hardly a rectangle in the building and the floor is below ground level.

On 17 June 1984, representatives of the Anglican, Methodist and Roman Catholic churches got together at St Bernadette's and signed an agreement or 'Declaration of Intent' binding themselves 'to God and to one another in the mission of Christ in this place.' Ecumenical services are held at regular intervals and although the parish church is next door, this unusual building must be included as a rare example of an ecumenical chapel brought back to life in recent times.

CHESHIRE

This is a county frequently travelled through, and yet off the main roads there is much to see. Climb the ramparts of Beeston Castle on a fine day and you have a wonderful view of the country from Wales and Shropshire to Chester and the land beyond. Many sandstone churches can be seen, although there are not so many small ones. As our first example I have chosen a Norman church, set outside its village in a field.

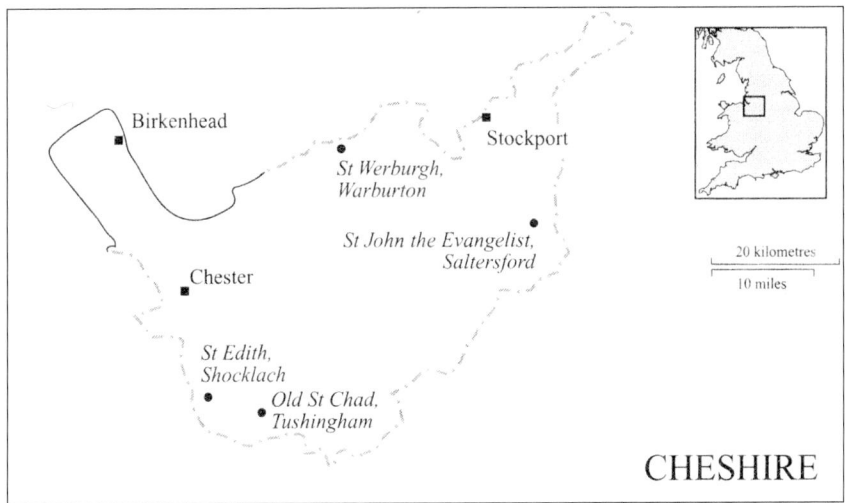

St Edith, Shocklach

Thirteen miles south of Chester and five from Malpas, Shocklach (no electric alarm system on the door handle!) is named after Thomas de Shocklach, who had a castle nearby. Enter by the Norman door and note the wooden floor has caused the bottom hinge to be close to it. The baptistery to the left is unusual, looking as if it had been made in a hurry. The font seems to be heptagonal, no side being equal in length. Above it are the arms of George III and a hatchment of the Puleston family. In the corner, five blocks up, is a small carving of a horseman with spear – presumably a hunter, which a notice says is similar to one at St Dochwys Church, Llandough. Was he a hunter or some mounted retainer of Thomas setting out for the wars with the Scots?

However, it is the ceiling that is a surprise. It is eighteenth century and is decorated with coloured floral bosses. This was paid for by the Revd Peter

Ravencroft in 1813 and has been recently restored. To celebrate the Millennium, a new window opposite the doorway has been inserted based on a design by local children. The east window looks as if it had originally been in a larger church and seems to fit badly. Outside, the two bells were placed above the west wall buttresses which had themselves been roofed over to create the baptistery. There are pews for 42 people, a nave of 32ft and, when I visited two ladies were busy cleaning for a wedding. Outside there is a small stable – for the Vicar perhaps – and many footpaths lead to the church although there is no sign of nearby cottages. To get into St Edith's, visit the church warden at White House Farm.

Other churches to see in Cheshire:

St John the Evangelist, Jenkin Chapel, Saltersford

Near Rainow, north of Macclesfield, the Jenkin Chapel is by itself on the Derbyshire border. It dates from 1733 and has a short saddleback tower of 1754. It has a chimney set in the south wall, square windows and box pews.

Old St Chad, Tushingham

Near the Shropshire border, Old St Chad stands in a field. It has been superseded by a new Victorian church. Built in 1689, it has the arms of King William III above the round-headed east windows. It has an oak font with a removable pewter bowl and the collection is done in a shovel dating from 1678. I must suggest this to our Vicar, as the discreet bags used in our church encourage foreign coins, buttons and the like.

St Werburgh, Warburton

A timber-framed church close to the Manchester Ship Canal. St Werburgh was a nun at Ely who was brought to Cheshire to run some nunneries by her uncle, King Ethelred. She is supposed to have brought a goose back to life and this creature is her emblem. The church is mostly Saxon, with a tower added in 1711. Now redundant, it is looked after by the Churches Conservation Trust.

CORNWALL

One of John Betjeman's favourite counties, Cornwall is full of small churches; alas many are not quite small enough. For example St Enedoc fits into this category. Granite is a favourite building material and many of the chapels or remains of chapels are also of granite. The Hermit's Chapel at Roche should not be missed for those who like a gentle rock climb and the chapel at Rame Head, also ruinous, used as a radar station in the war is a fine walk. Three little churches meet the requirements of this book.

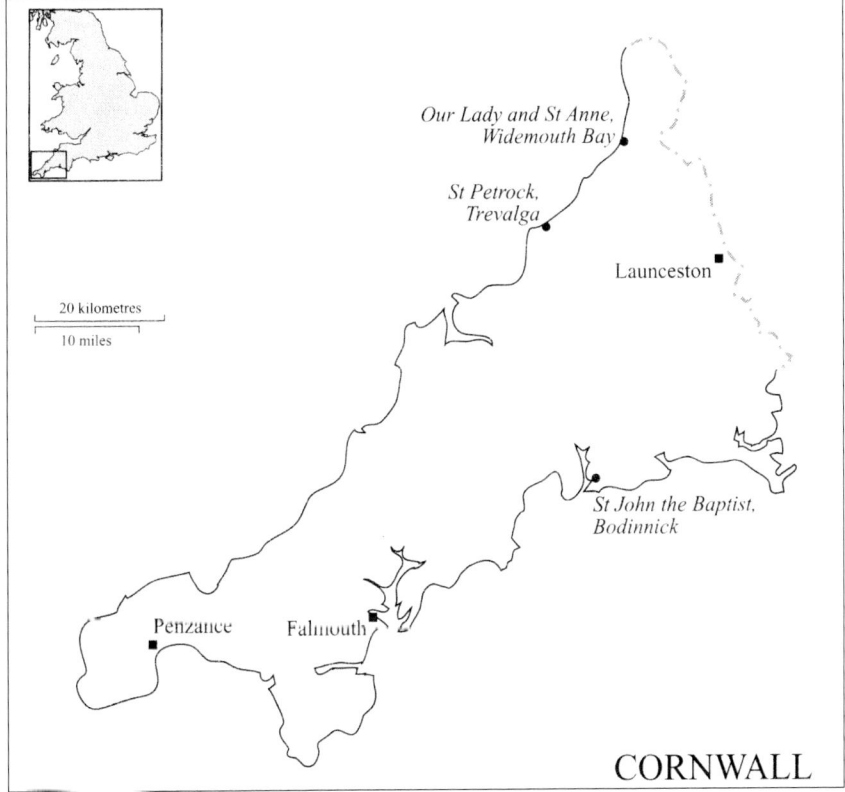

St Petrock, Trevalga

This is a little church that is hard to find. The village of Trevalga is midway between Tintagel and Boscastle and is a brisk walk from Boscastle along the cliff path.

The church is hidden from the road and well protected from sea winds by a wall. The tower has plain thirteenth-century battlements, with some remodelling dating from the fifteenth century. The entrance is up a footpath from the road – there is no car park – and then you are by the porch where there is a piece of carving (from the old screen) of a hand and a cloak. In 1875 the church was restored, but not too drastically, by J.P. St Aubyn.

The interior is chapel-like, well looked after and has a pulpit carved with scenes from the life of St Petrock – the saint with a stag, sheepskin and staff guarded by a wolf and a ship. The latter was carved in 1929 by a local man in memory of the former Lord of the Manor, Bolitho Stephens. The window in the tower is also part of his memorial. The east window has pictures of the Adoration, the Annunciation and the Ascension. The north transept is connected by a squint to the chancel. There are memorials to the Trehanes, Samuel Boscarrick and to the Revd James May (1832).

The last Lord of the Manor, Gerald Curgenven, presented the village to his old school, Marlborough College, on trust so as to preserve its character. Originally the patronage was in the hands of the Dean and Chapter of Exeter Cathedral and there is a chalice of 1576 which Pevsner describes as 'very pretty' – an expression he seldom uses.

This is not the smallest church in the country, but it is certainly one well worth seeing and supporting. The rector has seven other churches to look after including Minster in Boscastle and Forrabury on a hill near Boscastle. The latter has a plate to a young midshipman killed in the HMS *Glorious* disaster in 1940.

Our Lady & St Anne, Widemouth Bay

This church is a surprise. Firstly we went right past it without noticing it. Secondly, when we came back it turned out to be not only the smallest church in Cornwall, but probably one of the smallest in England. Inside, the nave measures 22½ft x 11½ft. There are 24 seats and no organ or piano. Part of the Poundstock benefice, it shares a vicar with Poundstock, Week St Mary & Whitstone. The original wood and asbestos building, not much more than a beech hut, stood in Madeira Drive, erected in 1929 as a private oratory for the Kingdon brothers. Then in 1940 it was placed in its present position. Later it was given a slate roof and tidied up inside. Now it is used for a regular communion service.

St Anne, mother of Mary, had her own cult which was popular, especially in Canada in the 1920s. Perhaps it is appropriate that at Poundstock – locked up but worth seeing if you can find the key – there is a trio of war graves to Canadian seamen whose ship, HMS *Regina*, was torpedoed off Trevose Head in 1944. Widemouth Bay also has connections with the USA, as it is the terminal of the main telephone cable between New York and Great Britain.

St John the Baptist, Bodinnick

Another small church in an unconventional building is St John the Baptist, Bodinnick, just a few yards up the hill from the car ferry. It was formerly a stable for the inn opposite. In 1948 the Vicar of Lanteglos discovered that there were some people who lived by the ferry at Bodinnick who wanted to attend evensong, but had no transport to get up to his church. The proprietor of the Old Ferry Inn gave him a room. The congregation grew and when Holy Communion was suggested, the innkeeper offered them the old stable. The hay loft was cleared out, the double doors of the garage end removed and a wall built. The hay loft became a vestry with an outside stair. The font, made by a Lostwithiel stonemason, was presented. A ship's bell was found and in 1994 the late Canon Goddard, who lived in Polruan, presented the Communion Set. In 1949 the church was dedicated to St John the Baptist by Bishop Holden. It seats 40 and is used most Sundays, some of the congregation coming over by ferry.

Just too large for the book is the little church of St Catherine Temple on Bodmin Moor, where the churchyard is a mass of wild flowers in the spring and what remains of the old church, just a few crosses and parts of sculpture, is attached to a little outbuilding by the door. It is worth a visit and one of my neighbours attends services there on her horse. I hope the latter is left outside for the sake of other members of the congregation!

St John the Baptist, Bodinnick, Cornwall © *Author*

CUMBERLAND

We have stuck to the old county boundaries, so that in the Lake District, Cumberland produces two small churches, one of which was known to Wordsworth and Tennyson and the other to all fellwalkers and climbers.

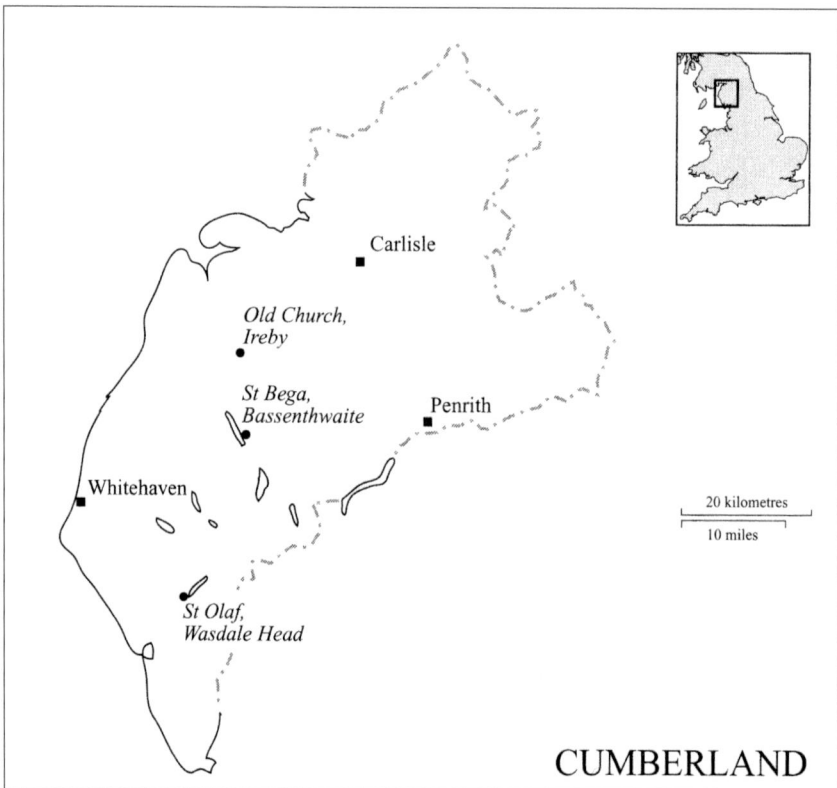

St Bega, Bassenthwaite

St Bega's Church is by the eastern bank of Lake Bassenthwaite and is approached across fields from the A591. St Bega was the daughter of an Irish chieftain. To avoid marriage to a Norse prince selected by her father, she fled to England and landed at St Bees. Her name lives on here with the Priory founded in AD 650 and the school. The Priory had her bracelet bearing an image of the cross as one of its treasures until the twelfth century.

The church, like Heath, Shropshire, started as a Norman two-cell structure, but was much done up by the Victorians; it has an hourglass stand, a monument to Walter Vane (d.1814) and outside a preaching cross and mounting block. Tennyson thinks of the church in his *Morte d'Arthur*:

> To a chapel nigh the field,
> A broken chancel with a broken cross
> That stood on a dark strait of barren land.
> On one side lay the Ocean, and on the one
> Lay a great water, and the moon was full.

The setting is still spectacular; oak trees, sheep, a stone wall and the solitary church perhaps standing on the site of St Bega's grave. You can come here on the first Sunday of the month for a 5.30 service (3pm in winter) or an 11am service on third Sundays. The team ministry also looks after Allhallows, Boltons, Ireby (small and worth a visit), Isel, Setmurthy, Torpenhow and Uldale.

Old Church, Ireby

This is the chancel only with a bell turret of a late Norman church which was made redundant when the new St James was built a mile away in 1847. It has three round-headed lancets in the east wall, and a churchyard with traces of Norman windows in the south wall. The Churches Conservation Trust look after it and recently two nave arcade columns were found being used as gateposts. They were removed to the churchyard.

St Olaf, Wasdale Head

This is the climbers' church, high up above Wastwater in the western Lakes, close to the Wasdale Head Hotel and surrounded by ancient yew trees. Mentioned in 1550, the church is a long, low building and only recently (1979) dedicated to St Olaf, a Norwegian king and founder of Christianity in Norway. He met a violent death, but is remembered at Trondheim Cathedral and in over 40 dedications in England and the Isle of Man.

The church seats 39, measures 35ft 9in and the Revd Bowers, Vicar in 1979, recalls the Bishop of Carlisle, a tall man, having to stoop to get under the beams in his mitre. The little church has plain oak seats with bobbin ends, old beams, a piscina in the chancel and an ancient silver chalice of 1565. There are Victorian iron brackets for oil lamps, so that on a cold winter evening the church would have looked like Captain Scott's party in his Antarctic hut. The walls are only 6ft 6in high. Outside there are graves to climbers, often including the words 'I will lift up mine eyes unto the hills' from Psalm 121. My late doctor and his wife, keen fell walkers, have a stone chair memorial in the churchyard which seems appropriate for those who knew them or for the weary climber.

DERBYSHIRE

A county of stones and green hills with many large mansions – Chatsworth, Hardwick and Haddon to name three – Derbyshire is well worth a visit. To see the smallest church though, you need to travel to Derby and a few miles out on the road to Ilkeston is the village of Dale.

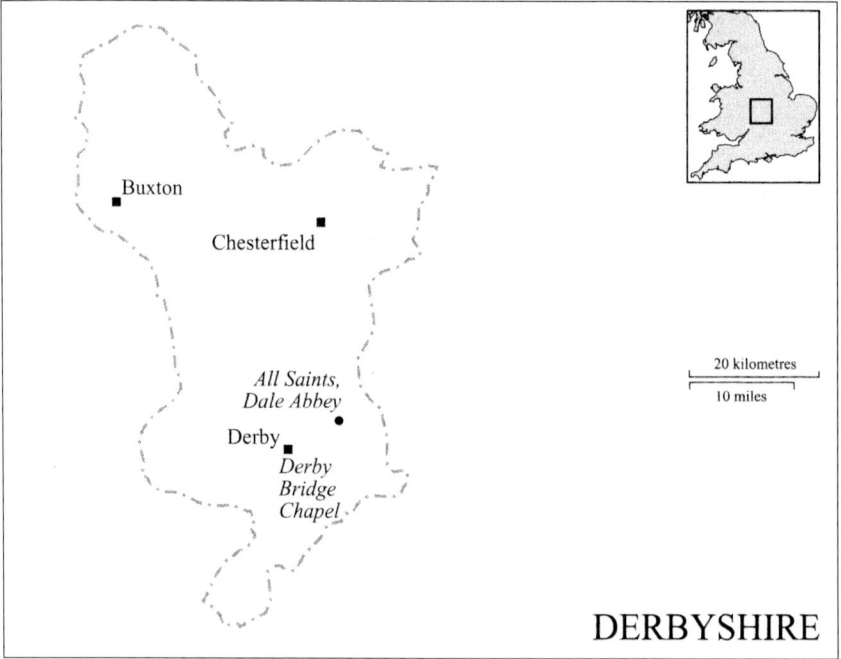

All Saints, Dale Abbey

You can be excused for not finding the church here, as it is past the manor house (where the church key is kept), then up a footpath through the churchyard to what looks like a farmhouse. The left-hand side of it is the church. Dale's grounds contain the ruins of a thirteenth-century Premonstratensian Abbey. In 1845, the infirmary, once part of the abbey ruins, was rebuilt in a farm building next to the church, with the gallery, approached from an outside staircase, being used for stretcher cases to see whatever they could during services. Much later the infirmary became a pub, The Blue Bell, and clergy used to change there before entering the church. Inside, as Jenkins says, the Mad Hatter reigns supreme. There is no proper altar, only a cupboard in front of the reading desk and the pulpit stands at a crazy angle with two candleholders at different angles. Maybe it was to allow compensation for a one-legged preacher? The Earl of Stanhope, whose tablet is on the south wall, has his 'Bishop's Chair'; otherwise there are box pews, with seats for about 40, two aisles, coat pegs and a wall painting of two saints embracing. There is a tablet to Dale's lay bishop inside and his throne is there, so some claim it was Derbyshire's first cathedral. In the past in became known as the Gretna Green of the Midlands as licences for weddings were issued without banns having to be read first. The floor space is 26ft x 25ft.

On the noticeboard was a notice for the special opening of **St Mary's Bridge Chapel, Derby** during September Heritage week. It is one of only six surviving bridge chapels in the country. Thanks to the Open Churches Trust, this chapel, dedicated to St Mary, is open 2-4pm, Tuesdays and Saturdays, from Easter to the end of September. Bridge chapels were constructed for the comfort of travellers and in perpetual memory of those who endowed them. There is one in Wakefield, restored in 1940 with a stair that goes to a tiny crypt and up to the roof. It was built as a chantry chapel to say prayers *ad infinitum* for its founder. The Derby Bridge Chapel dates from the fourteenth century and has been used by the Presbyterians, carpenters and as a store. More recently, in 1973, it gained an east window by Mary Robson and is used for regular Anglican services.

DEVON

One of the largest of our counties and in John Betjeman's words 'it is brightly coloured, more West Country than Somerset … less Celtic than wind-swept Cornwall.' I have selected seven churches, including one with a stiff climb, one a quaint survival and the third a chapel of note.

St Michael de Rupe, Brentor

This is a local landmark and not an easy church to reach. For a start you need a fine day and a head for heights – it is over a thousand feet up – as well as strong shoes, waterproof clothing and, if you wear a hat, make sure it is firmly tied round your chin. The top of the hill is windy and there are stories of the vicar approaching on all fours and the bride at a recent wedding been blown off the path into a bog. St Michael is usually associated with angels and maybe that is why this church is dedicated to him, like the ruined St Michael's on the Mump at Burrowbridge in Somerset. The first church here was built by Robert Giffard in 1130 and it has been repaired and cared for ever since. In 1319 it became part of the Benedictine Tavistock Abbey and inside the church are the coats of arms of the Giffards – three lozenges – and Tavistock Abbey's four rows of bells, blue, under two yellow stars on a red background. In 1912, the patronage of Brentor passed from the abbey to the Bishop of Exeter. Today it is used for evensong at 6.30pm in the summer when it is dry.

The little church sits in an Iron-Age hillfort with a few gravestones for the Batten family and one for Ingaret van der Post, widow of Laurens, who was born a Giffard. Inside the porch the visitor should pause and look back at the view before opening the heavy door. The low ceiling and white corbels give the effect of being in a ship. To cap this there is a sad monument to Percival Cocks, married in this church 11 August 1939, a Master Mariner, torpedoed in *RMS Navasota* on 5 December 1939 after barely four months as a husband.

The east window has a modern St Michael holding a sword in his right hand and scales of justice in his left. Like the St Michael in the Victorian church at Burrowbridge he looks in need of a good meal and a betting man would give the dragon a good chance in an even fight.

There is gas lighting, a font, four bells and a very cared-for atmosphere. At 37ft x 14ft 6in this is claimed by its guidebook to be the fourth smallest church in the country, seating only 36 people. The way down to the car park was easier and we found some large thistles, blue self-heal and the paler blue bugle flower. The field was full of cows all sitting down and we were back in the car park in 10 minutes, whereas the journey up had taken about 25. This is a church worth returning to for a service.

St Pancras, Exeter

Situated now just outside W.H. Smith at an odd angle, there must be some who think it should be removed stone by stone to a more sympathetic site. It was restored by Pearson in 1887 and now has regular services for shoppers.

St Petrock, Exeter

Found in the High Street, this church was called by Pevsner 'among the most confusing of any church in the whole of England'. It has a new chancel facing south, but the old chancel is still there, screened off. The church was restored, if that is the correct word, by the Harrison Sutton Partnership in 1985, and is still in use. Among the monuments is a relief of the Last Judgement by local sculptor Mr Weston.

St Stephen, Exeter

Found in the High Street with a chapel above an arch. It has a neo-Gothic interior of 1826. There is a modern tapestry by Bobbie Cox in the shape of a triptych behind the altar whose base forms the altar frontal. There is a Charles I coat-of-arms and some stained glass of 1946. Exeter was badly bombed during the Second World War so all the small inner-city churches have been restored.

St Mary, Honeychurch

The favourite of W.G. Hoskins, St Mary, Honeychurch is a real 'honey' of a church. Hoskins calls it a 'well-cared for country church', but lists it as poor. He means there is no sign of any money being spent on it. In fact, since he wrote in 1959, there has been an English Heritage sign put up (blown down in January 2002) and the tower has been rendered, the west door replaced and the hard-to-see Elizabethan coat-of-arms restored.

Honeychurch is a hamlet a few miles from Sampford Courtenay, with which it is united, and the Vicar, an Irishman, has to care for North Tawton and Bondleigh as well. We arrived on a cold January day just too late for the 3pm service, a sort of combined communion and evensong. There is no electric light so they had candles, a battery-driven keyboard (portable, fortunately) and one square paraffin heater. The church was built by Huna in the middle of the twelfth century. It is Norman, with a later tower and porch. Two interior corbels grace the inside of the porch. The font, with its zigzag designs is stone and unusual. Its cover does not fit and seems not to belong to it. The bench-ends, some carved, are medieval, but the box pews eighteenth century. There is one monument to John Dunning, 1773.

With a nave of about 29ft and seats for 40 (they had 80 with chairs brought in from a local farm for the Christmas carol service) and its narrow width, Honeychurch must be one of the smallest and certainly one of the most unspoilt churches in Devon. In the priest's doorway some pots were discovered in 1914 when it was unblocked. Pevsner thinks they were used for acoustic purposes, but it is more likely the local farmer's wife put them there and was pleased they became walled in as she had some nice new ones from the local market. In 1958, Colonel Shore replaced the east window, then in a bad state. It has been done so well that it looks much older than this. A word of warning to those about to put a contribution in the box here. If you drop it then it falls in between the floorboards and gives the Church Treasurer a difficult job to find. In 30 years of looking at churches I have never seen one with wider gaps between floorboards, but never met a friendlier congregation.

Nearby you can visit Sampford Courtenay where the 1549 Prayer Book Rebellion started and see a Devon church built of Cornish stone.

Loughwood Meeting House, Dalwood, Nr Axminster

Just off the main A35 between Honiton and Dorchester and 4 miles from Axminster, Loughwood belongs to the National Trust, but must be one of their least-visited properties. It is a Baptist house, first referred to in 1653 when the Baptists of Kilmington, scared of persecution, took to the woods and built their chapel in Lough Wood. The present chapel was erected in 1832 and before that they may well have met in the small farmhouse on the other side of the road. There is a gallery, high box pews, a high pulpit – the chapels were mostly preaching houses – and plain glass windows. At the back are two rooms, one with a fireplace, and outside a stable, so that both horses and the preacher could be fed and watered, plus any members of the congregation who had travelled a long distance.

There is a Baptist pool (for total immersion) beneath the floor in a central position with the table holding the bible. Take away the boards and there are three steps down to the water which came from a nearby stream. There is a clock made by John Tratt of Colyton which still works and a wall tablet to Revd Isaac Hann who was minister from 1747-1778. The nave measures 34ft and, although suffering from damp, one feels that the building could easily be put back to its original use today.

St Peter, Trentishoe

West of Lynton and close to the sea, this is a very small church, enlarged in 1861 when the chancel was built. It has a narrow tower built in 1638 that merges with the hillside. Inside, there is a musician's gallery where the visiting musicians have made a hole in the parapet so they could play the double bass.

DORSET

The majority of churches in Dorset are small. The Isle of Purbeck is worth a book on its own and the rest of Dorset would make Volume II. However, the smallest church is given by Pevsner as St Edwold.

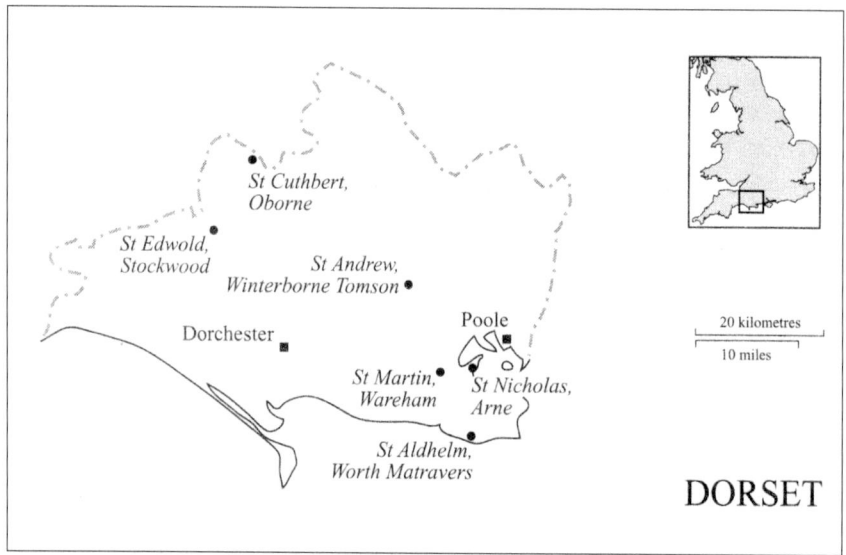

St Edwold, Stockwood

On the main Yeovil–Dorchester road, St Edwold can be combined with All Saints, Sutton Bingham (see p.113) and is alas also under the care of the Churches Conservation Trust. It is down a side road next to a farmhouse and approached over a footbridge. St Edwold was the hermit brother of St Edmund, the Anglo-Saxon king murdered by the Danes. Edwold is better known at Cerne where he lived near a spring called the Silver Well and Stockwood is derived from Stoke St Edwold.

There is no village, just a farm and a few farm cottages. The church measures 23½ft x 12½ft and seats 28. There is a brass and wood altar rail and a modern-looking font. In 1638 the porch was added and a stumpy little bellcote built in the same style as nearby Brympton D'Evercy. Alison Poole's drawing shows the bell rope which descends through the mouth of the gargoyle into the porch. One wonders how many people came flocking when they heard the bell.

The Bell Tower, St
Edwold, Stockwood.
Courtesy of Alison Poole

St Cuthbert, Oborne

This is the chancel of the old church at Oborne. The church was demolished and rebuilt in Victorian times. The chancel lay neglected until 1936 when A.R. Powys (see also Winterborne Tomson) restored it as a wayside chapel.

It has one pew, a sixteenth-century barrel roof and some medieval tiles set into the wall. The Ham Hill stone font comes from the vanished church of North Wootton and outside is the tomb of Robert Goadby, a printer who died in 1778 and a grave to Jane Highmore, 1844. The other tombstones have perished as the stones have crumbled. In the hedge there is a young elm tree. Let us hope it survives. This is a on a dangerous road (A30) and if you want to stop and see the building, care should be taken to find somewhere in the side road to the village for parking.

St Andrew, Winterborne Tomson

The third church in the area of the Churches Conservation Trust in Dorset is 8 miles west of Wimborne, off the A31 near a red crossroad signpost.

It is down a farm track and when we arrived two men were cutting the grass. Like Nately Scures (p.57) it is a single-cell building with an apsidal east end. The church measures 40ft × 15ft and has its original oak wood fittings of box pews, curved roof ribs and a very dilapidated gallery (unsafe). Some of Thomas Hardy's manuscripts were sold in the 1930s for A.R. Powys to proceed with saving this church, which the RCAM for Dorset calls Anderson Church after the nearby manor house. The church needs to be restored again and brought back into use.

St Cuthbert, Oborne. *Courtesy of Alison Poole*

Moving on to the Isle of Purbeck, the chapel of St Aldhelm, Worth Matravers, is 2 miles beyond the village and the last mile is only reached by a stony footpath leading to some cottages and the coastguard station. The chapel is a square building, like a blockhouse with buttresses, but it has a cross on the top and inside an altar across one corner, a central pillar covered in seventeenth- and eighteenth-century graffiti (was it once a prison?), a few old benches and a font. There are Norman ribs to each corner. Simon Jenkins relates how a father watched his daughter and her bridegroom set off by boat to their new home along the coast in 1140. The boat was caught in a storm and all drowned, so the father built the chapel in memory of the young couple. It has remained unchanged since and is used at Easter and a few Sundays in August. The village church at Worth Matravers has a tombstone to Benjamin Jesty who is famous as the first man to vaccinate successfully his wife and children against smallpox – his wife lived until she was 84 – and this was in 1796 and predated Jenner.

St Nicholas Church, Arne

St Nicholas, Arne

Not far from Worth Matravers the little church of Arne is one of the smallest parish churches in Dorset (you have to park in the RSPB carpark and walk into the village).

It measures 42ft and seats 50 with the average congregation in the 30s. There are steep steps to the door, but the church warden says that wheelchairs can enter by a special footpath round the back. The east window has a blue cross (removable during services when the altar cross is erected) and the font (rather high so the priest has to stand on the Rosie Evans stone to perform baptisms) has a font cover that is stored behind the curtain to permit those on the back bench to see what is happening. There are modern altar hangings by Kirsten Webb, a Book of Gifts with paintings of local wildlife, like the Dartford Warbler, and a picture of Alice Seymour, organist for 40 years who died in 1997 aged 95. *Arne* means 'A lone secret place'. Long may it stay that way.

St Martin, Wareham

The church of St Martin's is on the walls and had a gate next to it now demolished. It is basically a Saxon church with one aisle and is best approached via Lady's Walk through the trees. Inside (keys from Mr Joy, outfitter of North Street) there are 50 modern chairs and a modern portable altar rail and kneeler. The nave is 30ft long and the north aisle has a recumbent effigy of Lawrence of Arabia, 1935, by Eric Kennington. It shows a remarkably short man in Arab clothing. Lawrence spent the last years of his life at Wool in Bovington Camp and had a fatal crash on his motorcycle in 1935. He is buried at Moreton with a stone set up by Kennington, and the words 'The hour is coming and now is when the dead shall hear the voice of God'. One of the men at his funeral was the late King of Iraq, Ghazi I.

The glory of St Martin's, though, is the wall painting of St Martin as a soldier on horseback. He is shown giving half his cloak to a passing beggar. That night he had a dream in which Christ appeared to him wearing the cloak. This convinced him that the church was the career for him and he ended up as Bishop of Tours. The wall painting is twelfth century and is on the north wall of the church. When I was there a guide appeared and identified St Martin for us, which was both unexpected and helpful.

DURHAM

The county of coal pits and leek competitions is perhaps an unfair description of a county that boasts Durham Cathedral and its adjoining castle, both of which can be seen (and photographed) from inside a passing train. However, it has three wonderful Saxon churches. Two are at Jarrow and Monkwearmouth, but the smallest is in Escomb.

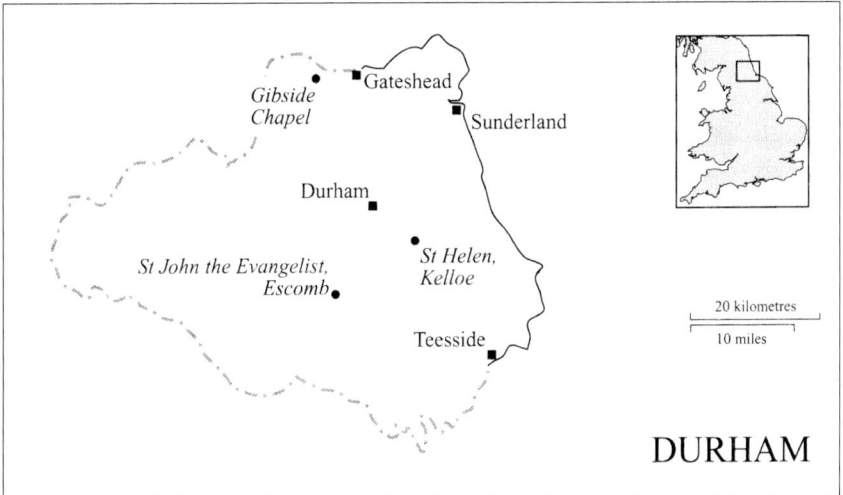

St John the Evangelist, Escomb

The best approach to Escomb is via the A68 to Darlington. There is a brown sign at Witton Park and after a few narrow roads and an up-and-down pit village there is the village of Escomb (Ed's Valley) with the church tucked inside a walled enclosure in the centre. The grass is cut, the keys are obtainable from No. 22 nearby and the lights are easy to find. Outside there are two sundials, stones that have come from Roman Binchester and signs of another building against the west wall. There is a small rosette on the west end of the north wall that might have been a Christian sacrificial stone.

Inside, the white walls, new seating and Millennium carpet (over the blocked north door) bring unexpected colour into the building. The Whiteheads, in their useful booklet, point out that the nave is three times as long as it is wide – 43ft 6in and 14ft 6in. The chancel is 10ft square and the chancel arch is a resurrected Roman arch. In Escomb village there was a Victorian church, but it was demolished in 1971 and the Saxon church was restored by Revd Lee (1959-64) and has been used ever since. The builders of what is considered England's oldest church must have known the right number of people to seat. There would appear to be no shortage of local churchgoers.

Outside, excavations in 1968 revealed a two-storey west annexe similar to the chancel and a north porticus entered from the chancel. Eight glass fragments were found identical to the Saxon glass at both Monkwearmouth and Jarrow. It is thought the annexes, never bound into the church stone fabric, were demolished and used for building the porch and wall in the fourteenth century.

Other small churches to see in Co. Durham:

Gibside Chapel

This has been a National Trust property since 1965 so is well signposted off the A694 between Consett and Newcastle-on-Tyne. The Bowes family (relations of the late Queen Mother) own the park and the ruined hall, but the chapel is occasionally used for worship. Designed as a mausoleum by James Paine in 1760, it was turned into a family chapel in 1812 and has appropriate fittings: box pews, a three-decker pulpit, blue velvet altar cloth – the altar being under the central dome – and an umbrella-like sounding board, so that even if it pours with rain, the preacher will keep dry.

St Helen, Kelloe

A small church, mostly Norman, off the B2291 between Cornforth and Cassop, Kelloe is built into the side of a hill. There is an Early English chancel refitted in 1901 by W.S. Hicks. But the most unusual item in the church is the medieval cross, one of the finest in Durham. It shows, in three tiers, Empress Helena searching for the Holy Cross and menacing Judas, who holds a spade, with Helena holding a sword. The island of St Helena was discovered on her feast day, which is 18 August in the West. In Ashton-under-Lyme church there is a series of 18 stained-glass panels depicting her life.

Also in Kelloe there is a tablet to Elizabeth Barrett Browning who was born in 1806 at nearby Coxhoe Hall. Inside, there is a grave marker stone with a cross set into the wall behind the altar. There have been some who object to the whitewashed walls, but personally I think they add light and must make it easier for worshippers to read the words in their hymn and prayer books.

ESSEX

Essex is a county of contrasts. It has some very small churches, made from red brick, wood, re-used Roman tiles and any stone that can be found. There is not space to do justice to them all here, so I have chosen five.

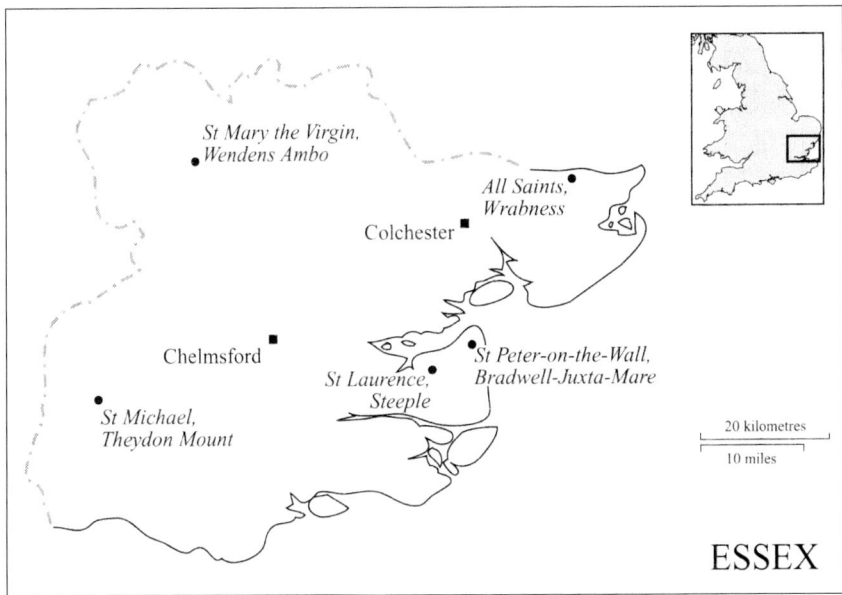

All Saints, Wrabness

Close to the Stour Estuary and a few miles from Manningtree, All Saints looks over to the Royal Hospital School at Holbrook. There is a bell cage in the churchyard similar to that at East Bergholt. Inside, it was a large flagon of cider, so maybe it was thirsty work ringing the bell.

The church is well loved inside. There is a hammerbeam roof that needs some angels, an octagonal font with some defaced figures of the evangelists and the south door has fleurons and shields in its fifteenth-century decorations. The chancel is fourteenth century and it seems its roof fell flat in 1697 and had to be repaired. Outside, the ground rises above the nave floor in places. The chancel has been battered like a castle using *septaria* mud and stone batters to stop any slippage. The builders of that hotel in Scarborough should have thought of this before the building slipped into the sea.

All Saints, Wrabness. *Courtesy of Richard Budds*

Among other small churches in Essex to see near Malden on the way to Bradwell is Steeple St Lawrence, a small Victorian church beside the road consisting of nave, chancel and belfry. The architect, F. Chancellor, has used bricks with brown stone and pieces from the previous church. There is a Second World War memorial monument that includes Flight Lieutenant Benn, brother of the well-known MP whose family comes from this area. The old church presumably had a steeple. Further on, the little church at St Lawrence was firmly locked, so on to Bradwell.

St Peter-on-the-Wall, Bradwell-Juxta-Mare

To get here is a pilgrimage. Go past the church of St Thomas and towards the sea. Leave your car at the small car park and walk for about half a mile to St Peter's. This was a fortified position, part of the Fort of Othona, a Saxon shore fort, with a wall to halt invaders. Some time in the period of Cedd, one of Aidan of Lindisfarne's missionaries, that is about AD 653, the first chapel was built here. Later, Roman stones were used from the fort to build a large chapel. The original building seems to have been a double monastery with square chambers for men and women each side of the porch. The latter had a bell. There was an apse like Billesley (see p. 128) at the east end and a square porticus each side of the apse. These have vanished though their foundations can be seen and the arch into the apse is clearly visible inside. At one time the chapel was used as a barn.

Today there is a modern altar with three stones set in it representing St Cedd's ministry. One stone comes from Lindisfarne, one is from Iona, where the Celtic mission to Britain began, and the third is from Lastingham, Yorkshire, where Cedd returned to build a monastery in 664 and where he died of the plague.

In July 1985, the Bishop of Chelmsford and the Bishop of Brentwood came here on a pilgrimage and consecrated the altar. Services are now held at regular times, the congregation seated on low benches. There is a regular pilgrimage on the first Saturday in July with 6.30 services in July and August, usually run by the chaplain, Revd Hugh Beavan of Bradwell Rectory.

On the way back from Bradwell, on a wonderful hot day in June, the two pillboxes were noticeable sticking out of the cornfield. They were built inland by at least 200 yards, for this was a defended beach in 1940 and the old Roman wall would have been covered in anti-tank blocks and barbed wire. St Peter's has an excellent guide book with colour photographs and a foreword by the Bishop of Chelmsford who writes, 'this is a very special place … as you spend time in this simple chapel, I hope that this guidebook will enable you to understand something of the great story that lies behind it, and the great God who is worshipped here.'

Other small churches to see in Essex:

St Michael, Theydon Mount

Not far from the M25, Theydon Mount church was rebuilt in 1611/14 after being struck by lightning. It was almost a private chapel to the Smith or Smyth family of Hill Hall. Inside there are no less than nine Smith hatchments and four Smith tombs. The east window by De Gleyn (1918) depicts St Michael between Joan of Arc and St George. There is a tiny black marble font and Mee reports that in the nave roof he saw a garland of flowers, an old tradition sadly meaning a bride had died before her wedding.

St Mary the Virgin, Wendens Ambo

Ambo so Canon Fitch tells me means 'both', as there were two Wendens, Great and Little, but the falling-down church at Little was demolished in 1662 and everything then concentrated on the picture postcard village of Great or Wendens Ambo. This is close to Saffron Walden and the Hertfordshire border. The tower has a Hertfordshire spike. At various times the church has been added to and what looks like a south transept is a nineteenth-century organ chamber. Various other additions were made – aisles and a larger chancel – so what might have been a tiny church is now a good size for its village. There is a sixteenth-century domed font cover, a fifteenth-century pulpit, a brass to a knight of 1415 and a tiger holding a glass on one of the bench ends.

GLOUCESTERSHIRE

There are three groups of churches to see in Gloucestershire, a county of contrasts. I used Cirencester as a base, and took the A417 to Gloucester, Ermin Street, and the first two can be seen in a morning.

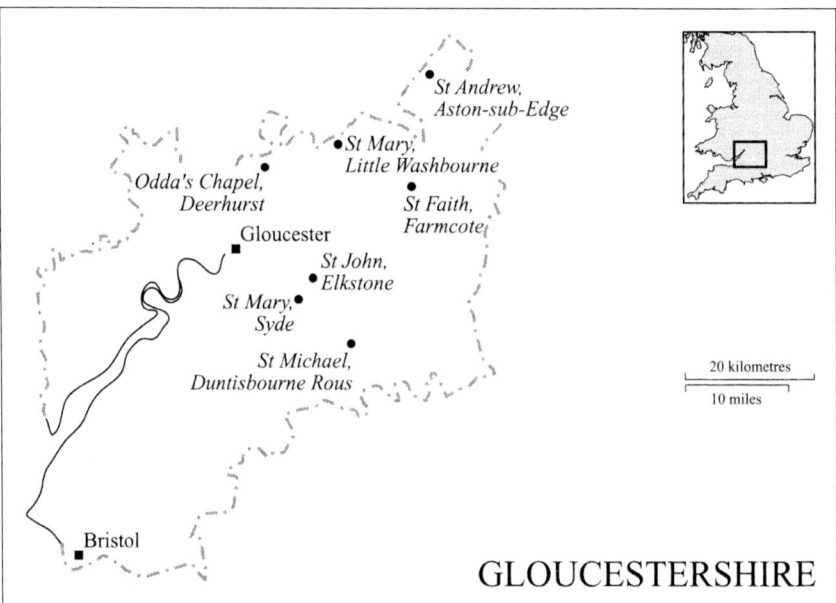

St Michael, Duntisbourne Rous

This is a small Saxon church with a Norman chancel and windows, built strangely into the side of a hill. The small saddle-back tower, common in this area, is Perpendicular with the upper part of it dated 1587. The porch is 1756 according to the date on the sundial. There is a Jacobean pulpit, a thirteenth-century font and choir stalls with misericords. Opposite them, there is some evidence of fourteenth-century wall paintings. All this is fairly normal and it is not until you go outside that you realise the most exciting thing is still to come. The crypt chapel is almost unique. It measures 16ft x 10ft, has a barrel ceiling and apparently two graves of previous vicars. It needs painting white, some small benches and a simple altar like St Apolline's, Guernsey (see p.25). It is certainly a holy place and I would like to see it used occasionally.

St Michael, Duntisbourne Rous, Gloucestershire © *R. W. Naesmyth of Posso*

St Mary, Syde

From Duntisbourne to St Mary's, Syde is a short journey. According to Domesday in 1086:

> Ansfrid holds Side and Turstin of him. There are 3 hides gelded. In the demesne are 2 carucates, one villein with the priest and 3 cottagers with one plough team and 6 serfs and 4 acres of meadow.

Today there are about 80 villagers and the parish is 628 acres. The floor has been raised, as in the old days it was mud covered by rushes – Thomas Muggliton's charity provided an annual fee of two shillings for two or three needy persons to change the rushes. The box pews are arranged in such a way that some of the congregation would have their backs to the vicar during the sermon and presumably nod off if it was boring. The badly defaced Royal Arms above the chancel are of Charles II, but the nave is eleventh century, the pews eighteenth century, the tower fourteenth century and the door fifteenth century with a fine iron ring.

St John, Elkstone

On the other side of Ermin Street is the finest Norman church in the county, as Pevsner says, 'best preserved and most interesting'. It is larger than Syde or Duntisbourne Rous, but should not be missed. The tympanum depicts Christ seated with emblems of the Evangelists. Inside, the east window glass is late twelfth century but the south window

Door handle at St Mary, Syde, Gloucestershire © *Author*

is very modern and depicts a young man with a footballer's haircut. Could the designer be thinking of the wrong St John? The Kop in Liverpool used to shout out 'Bring on St John' when their team was in trouble and this could be him.

The Norman arch is very fine with zigzag moulding, reflected by an inner arch of similar construction and an east window also with Norman zigzag pattern. The box pews are eighteenth century, but fit in well, much better than at Syde. There is a memorial to Judith Hooper who, when she died left her eight children to be looked after by her husband. I wonder how he coped.

The name Elkstone is nothing to do with a herd of drunken elk careering through the woods. It means the stone building of Ealac and there is a stone in the vestry with a tenth-century non-Christian design which may have something to do with the Elk Stone.

Outside there is a thirteenth-century tower with four gargoyles at each corner. One shows a man playing a cittern (like a lute) and another corner depicts a man playing a shawm, one of the oboe family. The tower replaces a demolished Norman tower which was built to replace a collapsed one that stood on the north side where its original base can be made out. Another unusual feature at Elkstone is the dovecot or columbarium created when the roof of the chancel was raised to that of the nave.

Norman double bellcote, Farmcote

North of Cheltenham I next stopped at the Hobnails Inn near Little Washbourne, St Mary, which was fortunate as they keep the key (marked 'I love Florida' on the ring label) and it is a 200 yard walk. Don't go beyond the church as fierce dogs await the unwary traveller. Inside, the fittings are all Georgian, although Pevsner calls this a Norman church with buttresses dating from the twentieth century. The wooden table altar has a marble top, there is a pulpit, sounding board and reader's desk, all in good condition, box pews, candle lighting and the rear pews are stepped up in a strange way so that those at the back can see what is happening. It is certainly one of the smallest churches in the county, unused, and in the care of the Churches Conservation Trust.

Carrying on from Little Washbourne, past the Hobnails Inn, there is, after a few miles, a turning right to Farmcote, a very isolated hamlet which seems to consist of two farms. Here it is easy to miss St Faith's, Farmcote, which seems to be the smallest church in the county.

It is a rectangular box, a nave with no chancel. This was demolished at an early date, excavated in 1890 and Pevsner states it was apsed like Nately Scures (see p.57).

There is a stone effigy to two of the Stratfords. Unfortunately the lettering, dating from the 1890 restoration, had red capitals and black letters. The red has now vanished so the words read like a cockney grammar: 'Ere lies Enry' etc. This is a Stratford tomb of *c.*1590. One Stratford was Lord Chancellor in Henry VIII's reign and there is an 1841 marble monument to Francis Stratford who died in that year.

In the walled churchyard, I spotted a short poem which sums up this most peaceful spot:

> The dawn of the Man for glory
> The Hush of the night for peace,
> In the Garden of Eve says the story
> God walks and his smile brings release.

After Farmcote there was a final church on my list, which involves going into Worcestershire, Broadway to be exact, now full of tourist shops and cars, out the other side and up the hill to St Andrew's, Aston-sub-Edge. This is a small Gothic church of 1796. The nave measures 32½ft and it seats 43 so it is not much larger than St Faith's, Farmcote. According to Pevsner, it was built by Thomas Johnson at the expense of the first Earl of Harrowby, whose family monuments are in the church. The prayer desk and lectern are from 1920 by Guy Dawber. The earls of Harrowby lived at nearby Burnt Norton, where the garden was the inspiration for the first of T.S. Eliot's *Four Quartets*. Strange that two of them should be composed around two of England's smallest churches.

The trainee reader, Peter Jackson, points out in his leaflet that St Andrew's is a farmer's church with special services for the farming year. It also had the last sexton in the diocese, Bert Ladbrook, who died in 1992. He used to ring the passing bell, one ring for every year of the deceased's life, a custom that has now sadly declined in most parishes.

Eliot must have heard the bell and entered the 'draughty' church for, as well as a thrush and a kingfisher, he writes:

> Time and the bell have buried the day
> The black cloud carries the sun away …
> Go, go, go said the bird: human kind
> Cannot bear very much reality.

The time was 1935 and the peace of Gloucestershire and of Little Gidding, then in Huntingdonshire, was fast evaporating.

Odda's Chapel, Deerhurst

This is a part of Gloucestershire that is quite different from the rest. Fisher describes it as part of the Saxon Kingdom of Hwicce – Gloucestershire, Worcestershire and part of Warwickshire. There was a monastery here (a few miles south of Tewkesbury) and the Celtic influence can be seen in the architecture of Deerhurst Church (well described by Simon Jenkins) and Fisher dates it from the early eighth century, just before Offa's reign and the Danish invasions.

After seeing this amazing church, complete with the dog Terri (on the foot of one of the brasses) and the angel outside facing the farm, walk down the lane to Odda's Chapel. This is an English Heritage property, but seems to be open at most times. In 1885, a half-timbered house was being repaired when plaster was taken off revealing an ancient window. The nave of the chapel had been used as a kitchen and the chancel had an intermediate floor. In 1675 a stone, now in the Ashmolean, stated in Latin that 'Earl Odda had this royal hall built and dedicated in honour of the Holy Trinity for the soul of his brother Aelfric which left the body in this place'. Bishop Ealdred dedicated it on 'the Second of the Ides of April in the fourteenth year of the reign of King Edward of the English.' This, Pevsner calculates, is 12 April 1056. It is a holy place, rather spoiled by a poet-admiral who has written at length about it in verse and put his poem on the wall. In summer this is a beautiful, calm place on the Severn. In winter, it is threatened by floods, hence the wall each side of the lane to the chapel.

Odda was a cousin of Edward the Confessor and Deerhurst is the 'forest of wild animals'. In fact, Deerhurst is more famous for farm creatures. In the church is a window to Edwin Strickland of Apperley Court. He went to America with the Cabot expedition and came back with turkeys, and it is a turkey cock that is the crest of the family. One is tempted to say the story of this place gets odder and odder.

N.B. There is a list of Gloucestershire Churches with opening details on the internet, which can be found under 'Christian Heritage' on the Gloucestershire County Council website.

HAMPSHIRE

The county has absorbed the style of its neighbours as far as church building materials are concerned. Thus we have the Hampshire/Sussex downland with the flint churches similar to those in Sussex. In the north of the county we have the Camberley and Aldershot town churches. In the west there is the Bournemouth area and the New Forest with gems like Minstead and Breamore. There are several small churches hidden well away, most of them very rural in spite of ever-increasing traffic and fast-growing townscapes.

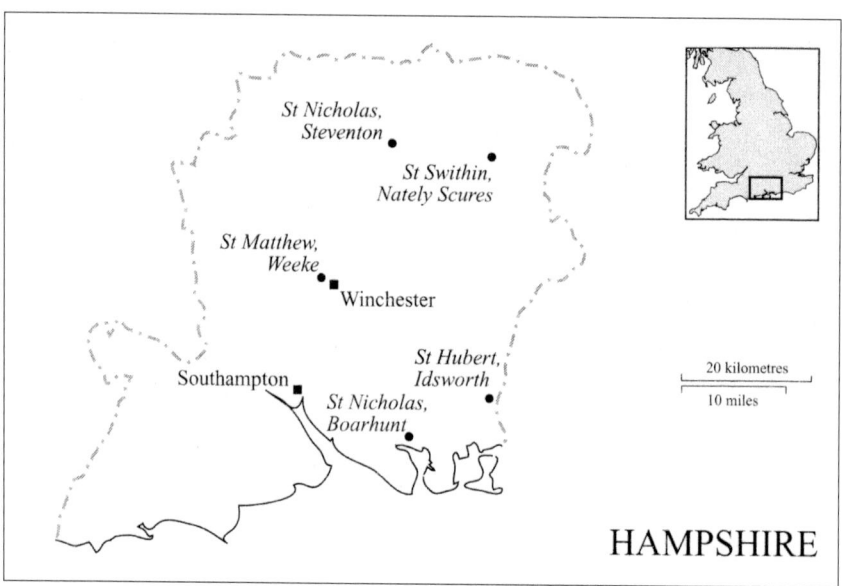

St Nicholas, Boarhunt

Standing next to a huge yew tree, Boarhunt Church can be found north of Portsmouth on a link road that leads down to the M27. It is a two-cell Saxon church with a simple bellcote and two blocked-up doorways to the north and south as well as a blocked priest's door on the south side of the chancel.

Inside – and the key is usually available nearby – there has been much recent restoration. The old black boiler, that used to get red hot on cold frosty Sundays, has vanished and there is a brand new organ. The guidebook plan shows the nave to be 32ft long and the north wall is slightly longer than the south wall.

There is a blocked Saxon window in the chancel and when I was there a vandal had broken two windows, one of which was in the squire's pew and had a coat of arms. Boarhunt is administered from St James-without-the-Priory Gate, Southwick, which is a Peculiar, the Rector being appointed by the Lord of the Manor and not coming under the Bishop.

There are two monuments, one to the Henslows with figures of Faith, Hope and Charity – the heads are believed to have come off when the monument was moved into the chancel. The other monument in the blocked-up south door is to Robert Eddowes, Store-keeper of the Ordnance at Portsmouth who died in 1765.

The church has no tower but a simple belfry. In size it is slightly larger than the smallest church in Hampshire, which is near Basingstoke, just off the road north towards Camberley. This is St Swithin's, Nately Scures. This is an apsidal church with a 28ft nave and an apse 16ft in diameter. The little church is constructed of flint rubble and door and window dressings of Binstead stone. Other apsidal churches in England are North Marden and Little Tey, Essex but these two have added vestries and porches.

St Swithin, Nately Scures

St Swithin is a lonely little church down a muddy lane by a farm. It is built of flint with a nave, chancel and apse all in one. The style is Norman and the bellcote is by Salvin, 1865, but in keeping with the rest of the church. The pulpit is also by Salvin and is made for a large cleric. The doorway has an arch with zigzag pattern.

Nately Scures was originally part of the manor of Hugh de Port, Lord of Basing. It then passed to the Earls of Northington and in 1786 to Guy Carleton, first Lord Dorchester. Sir Guy was an interesting character in British history. He served under Wolfe and became Governor-General of Canada in 1766. In the American War of Independence, some 70,000 loyalists were re-settled in New Brunswick and Carleton had to organise this so it is a church that Canadians should visit. On the south wall is a brass to General Thomas Carleton, brother of Guy, who was Governor of New Brunswick and helped Guy organise the resettlement.

Finally, there is the mermaid legend which is immortalised in a carving on one capital on the arch of the doorway. The story is that a young sailor met a mermaid and had a flirtation with her. On his return home, he fell in love with a local girl and, on the day of their wedding at Nately Scures, as they approached the door of the church, there was the mermaid sitting outside. She took the surprised sailor on her back and dived into the Water End stream (it must have been deeper then) then down the Lyde and the Lodden, into the Thames and out to sea. In the 1 May 1935 Jubilee number of *Punch* there is a different ending as both the local girl and the mermaid depart, leaving the sailor alone. However, the carving of the mermaid shows a little figure on her back, so the carver must have heard the first ending.

St Hubert, Idsworth

There is one other church which, larger than Nately Scures, is so isolated and interesting that it should not be missed. This is St Hubert's, Idsworth. Not marked on many maps, it is near Finchdean, in a lonely valley where the one road runs close to the main London–Portsmouth electric railway. Originally a chapel to the manor house of twelfth-century origin, it stands alone in the middle of a field. The first time I went there was to a christening and it was such a wet day that the baby needed an escort of umbrellas, but the wind meant that two hands were needed to hold them down and, had it been stronger, we would have had a Mary Poppins situation with umbrella and mother and baby being blown high in the air. The church has a brick porch, flint and tile nave and an added ugly chimney below the Sussex-style bellcote.

Inside, the church was restored by Goodhart-Rendel in 1912 when he was working on the manor house and he has done it so expertly that it is hard to work out what is original and what is not. The north nave wall has a Norman window and a blocked door. The twin-light windows in the south wall have pointed lights in wooden frames (like Wingham in Kent). There are box pews and a fine Jacobean pulpit. There is an eighteenth-century rail and a Goodhart-Rendel gallery which supports the organ.

However, the highlight is the fourteenth-century wall paintings that grace the north chancel wall. The upper picture denotes a huntsman carrying a bow going to a hunt with a white horse and hounds. There is a saintly figure, an armed knight and a hairy half-man, half-wolf creature. This represents St Hubert who cured a man who thought he was a wolf. The lower tier shows the life of St John the Baptist and Salome. The trees are bending with the wind as they did on the day of the christening and there is a small painting on the wall depicting the mural which helps with its interpretation.

In 1998, Idsworth PCC commissioned Fleur Kelly to paint a Millennium fresco. This depicts Christ in Majesty and in the background there is a white stag as Hubert, later Bishop of Maastricht, who was converted to Christianity when he saw a cross in the antlers of a white stag. The lady curate, Sandra Tebbutt, appears as she was in charge of the wedding of Mandy and Martin Banfield in July 2000, and the two bridesmaids, Ellen and Katy, appear too because the painting was in progress that summer. The boy on a bicycle is Timothy Fisk, the local farmer's son. Other means of transport in the picture are a steam train (for Derek, the organist), a tractor and trailer, a combine, a light aircraft and a Chinook helicopter. The inscription reads *MM in Die Sancti Fredericki* which means '2000 on the day of St Frederick' which was when the fresco was finished.

Idsworth, as so often happens in England, is not a village and scarcely a hamlet, but it has a devoted band of supporters for its little church. Long may it continue.

Other small churches in Hampshire:

St Nicholas, Steventon

This is Jane Austen's father's church and the family used to live opposite but the rectory has long since been demolished. It has nave, chancel and bell turret. It is early thirteenth century. To the left and right of the chancel arch are flat niches for lay altars. One has the remains of a wall painting. The chancel vault of plaster with wooden ribs looks nineteenth century and there is a monument to Anne Ausen (1795) and Revd James Austen (1819) which is by Hopper. For a few years we lived in an old cottage in Steventon and when stripping the paint off the kitchen door we found a mathematical table for teaching children sums at home. Maybe Jane had been there as a girl and it had been an infant school?

St Matthew, Weeke

This is a small church sideways on to the main Winchester–Stockbridge road. It is fairly low with nave, chancel and a bell turret. There is a Norman south door, Norman chancel arch and fragments of fifteenth-century glass in the windows. However, it is for the thirteenth-century paten (for holding the bread at communion) engraved with the lamb and cross and the Latin inscription *Cuncta creo, virtute rego, pietate reformo* that St Matthew is famous. It is one of the earliest known patens in the country. There is also a brass of 1498 to W. Complyn and his wife.

HEREFORDSHIRE

Many years ago, when I was a National Serviceman in Herefordshire, there was a fuel strike, but it did not put off the local farmers who drove into Hereford Market in their ponies and traps. We had to get the bus and were astonished that there was so much horse traffic around. Two churches from this rural county are of interest to us here, and I am indebted to John Leonard for mentioning the first, which is right on the Welsh border.

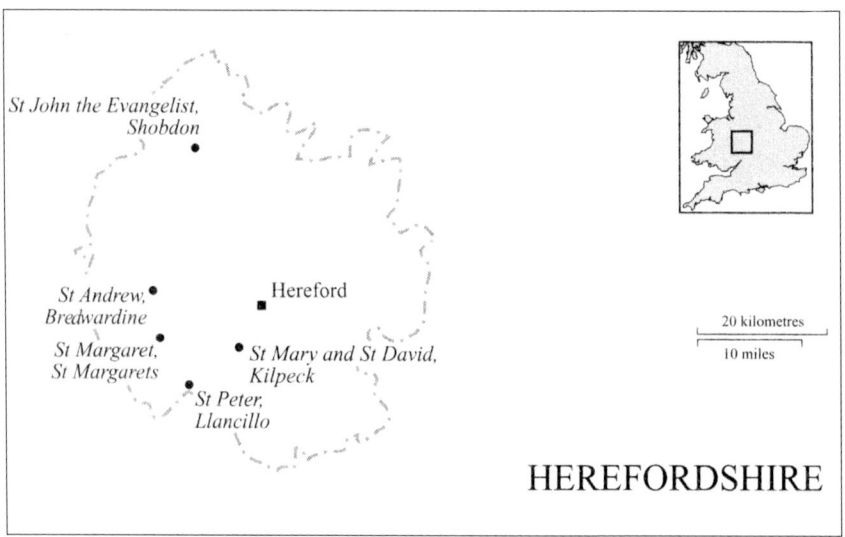

St Peter, Llancillo

To get to this church, you need to take the Hereford–Abergavenny road (A465) and 3.4 miles after Pontrilas, take a small bridge right, over the Monnow, turn right down a farm track, through three gates past cows and sheep, then under the railway, round a steep field into the farmyard (Llancillo Court Farm) where you will be greeted by dogs and geese. There is a 300 yard walk past the motte-and-bailey castle to the church.

Firstly, the door may seem locked but, if it is, the keys are hanging nearby. Secondly, the chairs were all stacked up when I visited in spring, with birds nesting in the surrounding yew trees and not a soul around. There had been a service that Sunday though, and the little building has two Norman windows and a sixteenth-century south window. The panelled pulpit dates from 1632 and a 'dugout' chest is supposed to be there, but I did not see it. The nave is about 36ft long and on the Prosser monument, which included Laura who died in 1973, is the opening line of that famous hymn: 'The strife is o'er, the battle won'. One hopes it does not spell the end too of this atmospheric little church (see p.152).

St Margaret, St Margarets

Not too far from Llancillo – you go up the road to Pontrilas and through Abbey Dore, then turn left to Bacton to a T-Junction where you turn right to Newton, then right again up a hill to the hamlet of St Margarets. The church is on the left behind a hedge. It is simple outside with a board bell turret that overhangs the gable. The glory of the church is the Rood Screen, of about 1520, which stretches across the nave. Supported by two posts, carved with empty niches, it has a mass of carvings all now silver-grey in colour. The nearest similar screens are in Wales at Llanfilo, Llananno and Llanwnnog. The eighteenth-century texts have been restored so one can read them easily:

> Cry aloud, spare not, lift up thy voice like a trumpet, and shew thy people their transgressions and the house of Jacob their sins.
>
> *Isaiah* Chap.57 v.1

This is one of them, chosen perhaps by the choirmaster. This is a well-loved church and worth discovering.

Other churches in the county to visit are:

St Mary & St David, Kilpeck, for its carvings, and St John the Evangelist, Shobdon, for its Walpole gothic interior. The Church Conservation Trust has no less than eight churches, most of which are small and very rural. St Andrew's, Bredwardine should not be missed too by Kilvert enthusiasts, for the nineteenth-century diarist is buried in the churchyard here where the road crosses the Wye.

HERTFORDSHIRE

Hertfordshire is a county I should know well, having spent five years at school there. My father attended Sarratt Church, a village later associated with George Smiley's spy debriefing house. Small churches were everywhere but I am indebted to Mrs Kelsall of St Albans for three of those selected.

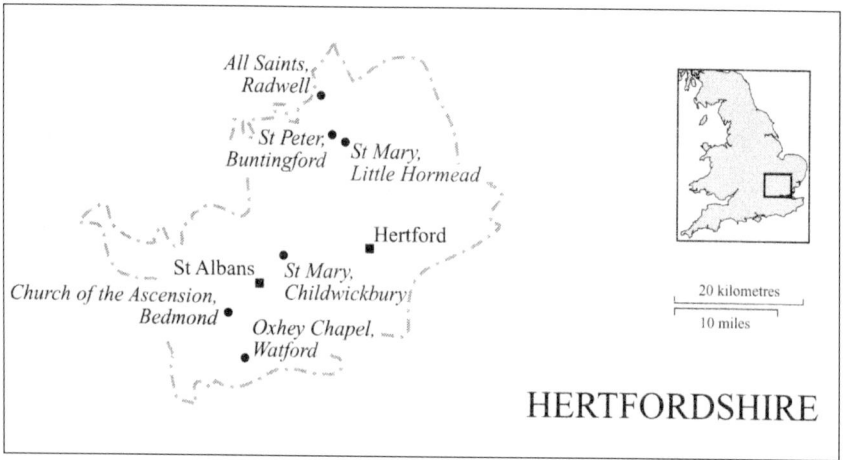

Church of the Ascension, Bedmond

This is a tin tabernacle, which was purchased in 1880 by Mr and Mrs Solly of Abbots Langley and came in pieces by rail (probably to Kings Langley). It was revived in 1983 as the local church and although it measures 50ft x 19½ft, has a wood lining and seats 64. The east window is modern, showing Christ preaching to the multitude.

The church is painted white with a tiny black and white spire. Bedmond is a mile from Abbots Langley, which was well known in my youth as the home of Ovaltine (1931).

St Mary, Childwickbury

This is slightly larger, Victorian (1867) and was constructed as an estate church and school combined. It has a very devoted congregation who were preparing for a concert when I arrived and assumed I was a trumpet player. The building is unremarkable, being constructed on this private estate by Sir Giles Gilbert

Scott and containing sad monuments to the daughters of Sir Blundell Maple (of Maple's furniture store) who lived in the big house. The two girls died of scarlet fever in the 1890s.

The church is approached through large gates and one has to park and enter round the back. The key-holders at No. 12 were most helpful. The place is pronounced 'Chillickbury' so no-one in St Albans I asked had ever heard of Child-wick-bury. This reminds me of our Bishop, promoted to Bury, who went on a reconnaissance trip to Suffolk. He arrived in Bury, saw two men coming up the hill, one carrying a spade, the other a rolled-up carpet. 'Where am I?' he asked. 'I don't know where you be' said one of the men, 'but Fred and I we come to Bury St Edmund.'

All Saints, Radwell

A few miles north of Baldock, Radwell is mostly Victorian, measures 35ft 16½ft in the nave and 20ft x 13½ft in the chancel. Inside is a fine monument to Sir William Plomer (1625) in armour at prayer. The church warden, who wrote the excellent guide book, looks after the key and lives in the Mill House nearby.

This is a small church, mostly nineteenth century, without a tower but with an arch at the west end of the nave as if the builder had intended to build a tower. Inside there is a carved Royal Arms, a three-light east window of 1500 and a fifteenth-century font. Outside there are four mass dials, one of them upside down – for Australians to tell the time, perhaps?

All Saints, Radwell, Hertfordshire © *Author*

Other small churches in Hertfordshire:

St Peter, Buntingford

This is a compressed cruciform church of 1614 with an added 1899 porch and apse – a mistake, says Healey in his Shell Guide. The old church outside, St Bartholomew, is a ruin, but the chancel was still being used as a cemetery chapel.

St Mary, Little Hormead

A few miles east of Buntingford, Little Hormead church is cared for by the Churches Conservation Trust. It has an eleventh-century nave, a Norman chancel arch and one of the original Norman doors is preserved inside. There is a fourteenth-century font, a Charles II coat of arms and some ancient timbers supporting a later bell-turret.

Oxhey Chapel, Watford

Two miles south of Watford on the B4542, Oxhey Chapel was built by Sir James Altham in 1612 of brick and flint with straight-headed Perpendicular four-light windows. It has its original west door, a fine late seventeenth-century font and cover. The communion rails and seating date from 1897, but are well done. The chapel is cared for by the Churches Conservation Trust and the key is nearby. Oxhey can be reached by train from Euston to Watford and then by bus.

HUNTINGDONSHIRE

The county of Cromwell and, strangely, of John Major, is now tacked onto Cambridgeshire but I have included it separately with the old Soke of Peterborough. There is only one candidate for the smallest church.

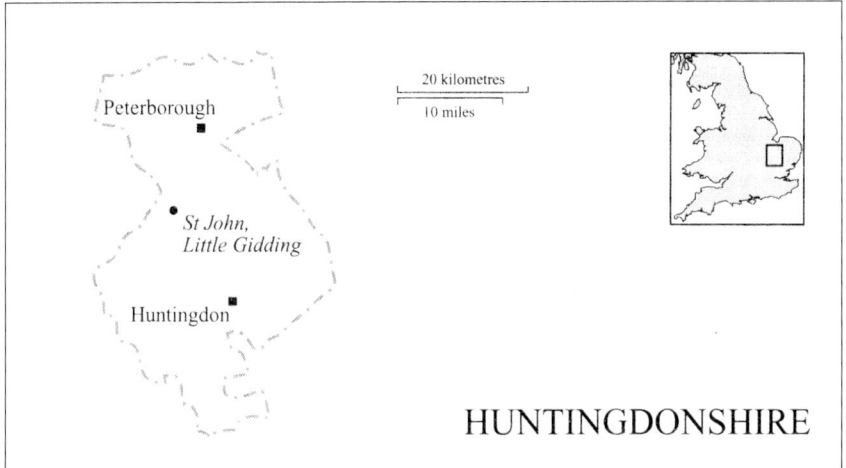

St John, Little Gidding

This is Nicholas Ferrar's church, which he built for his community when he became a deacon in 1626. With his brother and family and a community of about 30, he had a school and an Anglo-Catholic discipline, with three services a day, work on concordances of the bible, bookbinding and embroidery. It lasted until 1646 when Cromwellians attacked it as 'Popish' and it came to an end. The church was restored in 1714 and again more recently. It looks like a college chapel inside, with a barrel ceiling, wonderful chandelier and candle lighting. The candle sconces date from 1920 and are by W.A. Lee, and the lectern is fifteenth century – a present perhaps to Ferrar by another church? King Charles I came here on his final trip to surrender to the Scots, T.S. Eliot came here in May 1936 as war was approaching and based his final poem in his *Four Quartets* on Little Gidding. He wrote his poem in 1941 during the war:

> If you came this way in May time, you would find the hedge
> White again, in May, with voluptuary sweetness.

He seemed to find some sort of halt in time here:

> Here, the intersection of the timeless moment
> Is England and nowhere. Never and always.

For Eliot, his holy places were Burnt Norton near Aston-sub-Edge and above all other places, Little Gidding.

ISLE OF MAN

An island the size of Rutland, but with hills like Cumbria, and weather and coastal scenery like Cornwall. I had two wet days there and one glorious day I left. The clergy were extremely helpful and I found two small churches, both in excellent shape, well used but hidden on the west coast. The parishes (17 of them) have names beside the road and the work of Manx/Gothic Revivalist John Welch is evident. He was commissioned by Bishop Ward in the 1830s to design a combined schoolhouse and church at St Luke's, Baldwin and a smaller one at:

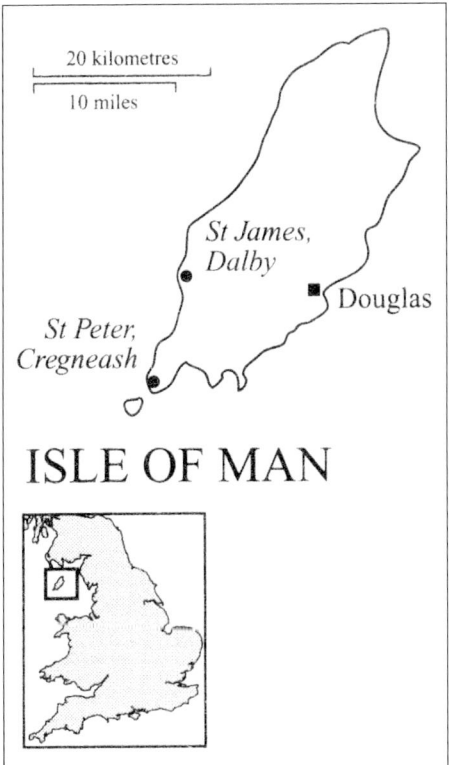

St James, Dalby

Dalby village is between Port Erin and Peel. It is merely a collection of cottages with a farm or two overlooking the sea. The church-cum-schoolhouse – the school was closed in 1932 due to a shortage of pupils – is strangely seated within.

There are pews seating 18 facing the altar and a further 18 seats sideways on, with space for the organist on the other side, and curtains to pass through to the old schoolroom and kitchen. The floor measures 16½ft x 24ft with the narrow part lying between the altar and the wall of the schoolroom. There is a small wooden font and the communion vessels consist of a chalice, two plated alms dishes and a Sheffield plated flagon presented in the 1920s when there were 31 boys and girls with Cecil Collister, the teacher. The guidebook gives the name of every pupil. I was fortunate to meet a local electrician who let me in – St James was the only locked church I came across.

St Peter, Cregneash

This is a little one-room church, seating about 40, in the last village you reach en route to the Calf of Man. It is next to an old Manx farm with threshing machine, thatched cottages etc. which is open to the public. There is a green phone box and a Victorian red letter box in the wall, but the church is well used. Inside, the Book of Common Prayer was evident and the hymns (A & M) announced were 242, 255, 290 and 192. The windows have local decorations – fish, stooks of corn, a thatched cottage and the two round west windows have red glass which creates an interesting light. Outside there is a Manx cross in the little garden – no graves to be seen – and a list on the noticeboard states there are seven sidesmen and two sideswomen. Holy Communion is on the first Sunday but evensong on other Sundays, so a Lay Reader would be useful. It has a most friendly atmosphere.

Other small churches visited were Old Kirk, Ballaugh which stands on a keeill site (see Glossary) with a font in its window-sill, and St Mark in Malew which has slate tiles, an 1899 apse and east window, organ gallery and strange sliding wooden slats in the window for ventilation. There is also a small chapel inside Castle Rushen no longer used except for the machinery of the castle clock.

ISLE OF WIGHT

The Isle of Wight is roughly the same size and shape as Singapore but there the resemblance quickly ends. It is still reasonably easy to get about and, out of season, is a delight.

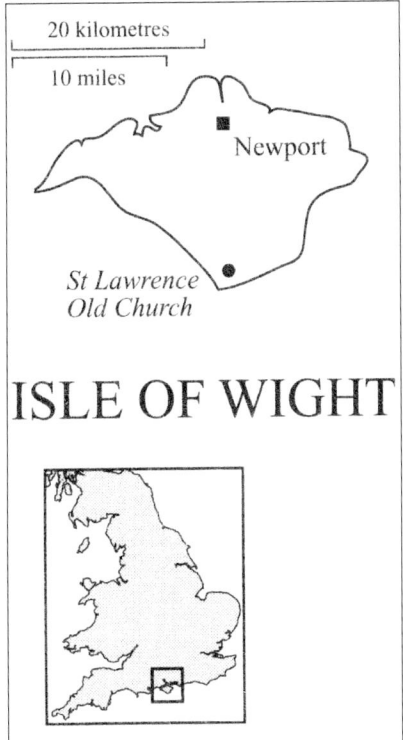

St Lawrence Old Church

This is easily the smallest church on the island and was once the smallest in England (20ft x 11ft). However, in 1842 the Hon. C.A. Pelham, who had inherited the Worsley property that included St Lawrence (on the southern tip of the island), put up a new chancel and porch. Mostly built at different dates, the church has two-light windows, four of them on the south side. The porch arch is pointed like the small bell arch which houses the solitary bell. There are trees all around and it must be a haunted place to visit at night.

St Lawrence Old Church. *Courtesy of V. Vivian*

The original church was built as a memorial chapel to the de Aula family, but it became a parish in 1305. In 1878 the Victorians, perhaps encouraged when Tennyson and his friends came to live on the island, decided instead of enlarging St Lawrence, to build a new church designed by Sir Giles Gilbert Scott, which Pevsner describes as 'indifferent, especially internally', but which does have some pre-Raphaelite glass in it that came from a closed-down hospital in Ventnor.

Victor Vivian includes St Lawrence in his five-mile walk guide from St Mary & St Rhadegunde at Whitwell to Old St Boniface, Bonchurch. The last part of the walk is along the coast to St Boniface's church. Here the poet Algernon Charles Swinburne is buried in the churchyard. In the churchyard at St Lawrence, the only headstone of note is to one of the relations of Walt Disney.

KENT

Some years ago I attended the Readers' Conference in Cambridge where we all sat in a hot lecture room to listen to a learned talk on St Augustine. Alas, it was St Augustine of Hippo and not St Augustine of Canterbury. I asked the lecturer at question time, perhaps rather rudely, if he had spoken on the right man as surely the latter was the more important of the two to English Christianity. I don't recall the reply, but the Kent contingent thanked me afterwards as they had been convinced that our lecturer got the wrong man.

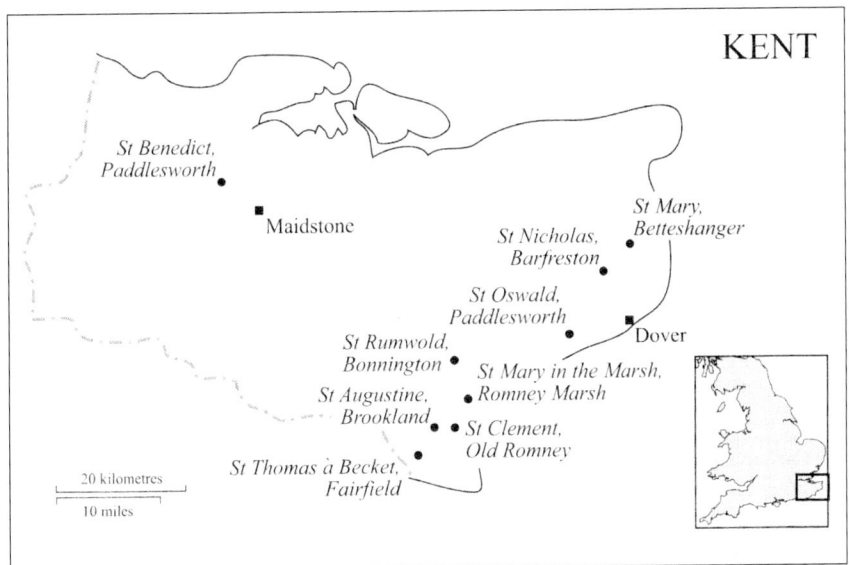

It was in AD 597 that St Augustine (of Canterbury) came to Ebbsfleet with his 40 men to convert people of the area to Roman Christianity. It already had Queen Bertha, a Celtic Christian, so the idea wasn't new. Ebbsfleet, which has the flying bishop today for communities like Charlestown, Cornwall, that do not accept women priests, was then on the island of Thanet. If he burnt his boats to keep warm, as some say, he was in trouble, as there was no way over from Thanet to the mainland without them. When he did succeed, perhaps in the one boat remaining, he landed at Richborough Roman fort and then went down Watling Street to Canterbury where he was greeted by Bertha and King Ethelbert. The latter had already been out to meet Augustine under a tree so that he was happy to be converted to Christianity at a later date. St Martin's Church, near the prison, is the oldest church in Canterbury and is where Bertha and Augustine worshipped together. Today it is too large for our list, but well worth a visit.

St Benedict, Paddlesworth

The smallest church in Kent is probably St Benedict, Paddlesworth, which is in the Rochester Diocese. It is 45ft long and 17ft wide. The chancel is about 15ft, so the nave is 30ft long, but difficult to measure. This is a Norman church with a fine doorway, tie beam roof, wrought iron chandeliers and some village hall-type chairs. The two settles in the guidebook have gone and there is much damp. The caretaker opposite (who has fierce dogs) was doing her best to keep the building dry and said the east wall had been rebuilt after a lorry crashed into it. St Benedict is now (since 1976) in the care of the Churches Conservation Trust.

Nearby, but only open on Sundays, is Dode Church, a small ecumenical building on Holly Hill.

St Nicholas, Barfreston

There are two other churches in Kent which are much more worthwhile visiting and both of them are small. The first is Barfreston, a two-cell building some 6 miles out of Canterbury off the A2, built on a hillside and seemingly at an angle. It has been called the Kilpeck of the south as it has some remarkable carvings. In size it is 4ft longer than Paddlesworth, but much the best church in Kent for twelfth-century carving.

Barfreston has its bell attached to a small rocking beam fixed on the yew tree. The tree itself is older than the church, and in 1885 Archbishop Benson rejected a plan to add a roof belfry to the church so the PCC placed their bell in the tree where it remains today and is used every Sunday to summon the faithful to prayer.

On the south door there are animals fighting, men on horseback and a seated bishop, and signs of the zodiac. On the tympanum is Christ with angels. Inside there is a band of decoration below sill level with recesses each side of the chancel arch for altars. There is much zigzag and dogtooth engraving in Caen stone. There are few monuments and the east window is dedicated rather surprisingly to the memory of Jane Austen. However, this is the wife of the Revd Edward Austen, another Jane, and not the famous authoress. Edward was the great nephew of the creator of *Pride and Prejudice* and she came to see him once when staying at nearby Ratling.

If you find there are no postcards or guidebook do not despair, near the pub is April Cottage and both are on sale here. The red guidebook goes into much detail about the carving and is worth obtaining.

The other church to see is on the Kent/Sussex border and is one of many churches on Romney Marsh worth a visit.

St Thomas à Becket, Fairfield

Fairfield is an isolated building in the middle of Walland Marsh not far from Brookland. The church is dedicated to St Thomas à Becket. To reach it, you first have to get the key which is kept on a nail by the back door of the nearby Becket Barn Farm. There is a five-minute walk on a causeway through the sheep field. In the 1960s the church was often standing in flood water, but since then the drainage has improved and a boat is no longer required. What we see today is Caröe's reconstruction of a medieval church carried out in 1912. It is timber built, originally lath and plaster, but replaced with bricks in the eighteenth century.

Inside, there is a low ceiling, dark appearance and no electric light. The box pews are painted white and there is a tile floor. There is a triple-decker pulpit with a note on the 'ping-pong bat' information guide saying that no-one of ample girth should apply for post of clerk, as the seating position below the pulpit is very small. The altar rails are three-sided (to prevent animals fouling the little altar) and they too are painted white.

Caröe used as much of the original material as possible in his reconstruction and the building, like all the Marsh churches, is in excellent condition. The church seats about 40 and the nave is 42ft long to the altar rails. Services are held regularly and Fairfield must qualify for the smallest Kent parish church in regular use.

The Romney Marshes Historic Churches Trust has a useful list of access arrangements, which other associations could copy. For our trip to the Marsh churches – I had a local guide – we started at St Mary-in-the-Marsh, a small Norman church with a fine George III coat-of-arms, a scratch dial and, outside, the wooden gate-style monument to E. Nesbit, author of *The Railway Children*. From there we went to Old Romney, St Clement, where the floor showed distinct green signs of recent floodwater. The box pews here are painted pink, there are twin hagioscopes and a ladder for access to the tower marked 'dangerous'. One hopes that there is a safer one for those who have to get up to the tower. The font has four legs, with animal carvings just visible on their capitals. There are seventeenth-century commandment boards behind the altar and a triple-decker pulpit.

From Old Romney we went to Brookland St Augustine. This is a large church with an impressive round-carved lead font dating from the twelfth century. The 60ft external bell tower, tiled in three parts, looks like an agricultural building for drying hops. Crossing into Sussex after Fairfield there is St Mary, East Guldeford. There are nine other churches on Romney Marsh, easily accessible, but to see a nearby church not quite on the marsh, we went to **Bonnington, St Rumwold**, a popular church famous for its Christmas candle light service and shown on the front cover. Pevsner describes it as sitting 'like a plump little grey hen on the bank of the Royal Military Canal'. It is stone, with a Norman chancel and a Perpendicular north porch. There is a weatherboard turret and a lead cupola dating from the seventeenth century. It has a triple lancet window behind the altar, an eighteenth-century pulpit, a circular font with an unusual cover and the only thing spoiling the interior is an ugly heating pipe next to the pulpit and its sounding board. St Rumwold was born at Kings Sutton in Northamptonshire and lived only three days, but in this time he stated 'I am a Christian' three times and preached on the Trinity. He is buried at Buckingham, but the fishermen of Folkestone adopted him as their patron.

For information about the Romney Marshes Historic Churches Trust, contact their Membership Secretary, Mrs J. Campbell, Pippins, Sandhurst Cross, Hawkhurst, Kent, TN18 5NU.

Other small churches to see in Kent:

St Mary, Betteshanger

Just off the A256 Sandwich–Dover road, Betteshanger was restored by Salvin in 1853. Its north doorway has genuine Norman sculpture with some zigzag moulding. There is a tiny figure of Christ with a large head. Inside there is the Royal Arms of William III and some stained glass by Kempe. There is a 1740 monument to Admiral Morrice by Scheemakers showing carvings of ships and cannon.

St Oswald, Paddlesworth

Not to be confused with the other Paddlesworth, this one has a 40ft nave and is a Saxo-Norman church high on the cliffs above Dover. It has a tiny piscina, a very small east window, three small Norman windows and a red-brick floor. It is a sister church of Lyminge so may have known the famous Queen Ethelburga, who helped bring Christianity to Kent. The seventh-century group of Kent churches includes St Mary and St Ethelburga (daughter of King Ethelburt), Lyminge and the abbey church at Reculver. In 1085 the body of St Ethelburga was brought to Canterbury and rested at various churches en route – maybe St Oswald, Paddlesworth was one.

LANCASHIRE

The south of the county is industrial and crowded, and in the north it runs into the Lake District so it makes a hotch-potch of architecture – the most difficult county Pevsner says he has had to describe. Thanks to the Blackpool and Liverpool Diocesan offices, however, there are no problems with small churches.

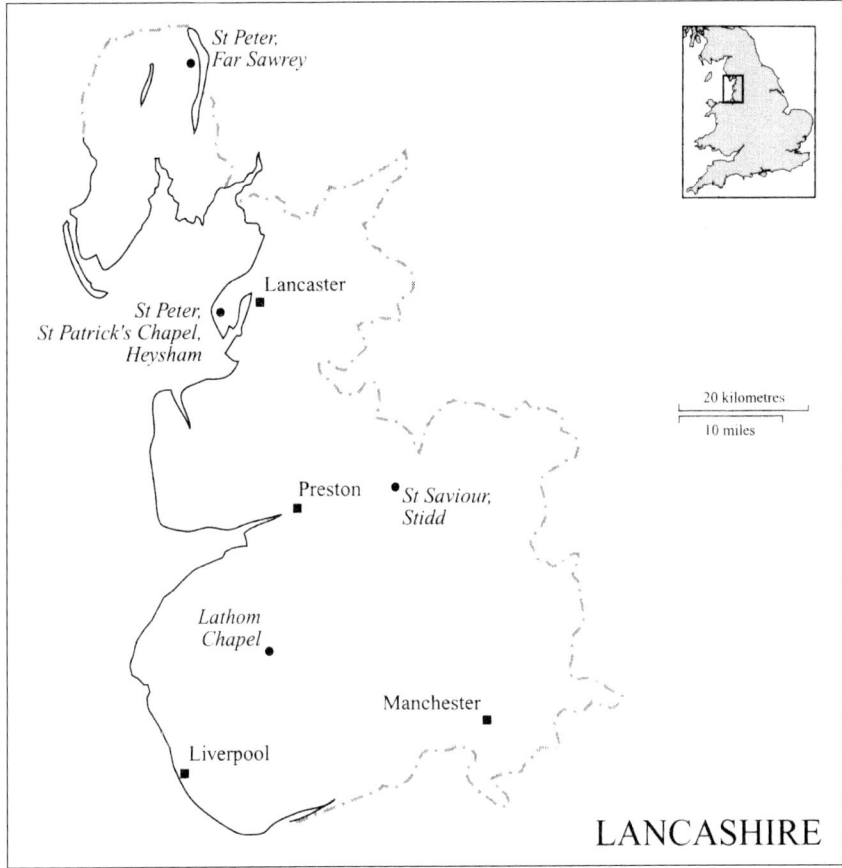

St Saviour, Stidd

To find this little building, leave the M6 at Junction 31, take the A59 towards Clitheroe and turn off on the B6245 towards Ribchester. There is a large sheep field on the right and the church is at the top end of this down a stony track. It was founded at the time of Becket by the Knights of St John and is a one-room structure, with an Early English south doorway, two Norman windows on the north wall and a blocked-up west door high up that must have been an outside entrance to a wooden gallery. The eight-sided font has five bulls, a lion and what looks like a rampant rabbit, but may in fact be a lion. All are carved in a heavy primitive manner, but as it was harvest time the font was well decorated, so difficult to see without destroying the decoration.

There are rude benches and about 40 chairs had been put out for harvest. An old door lies against one wall, but the most surprising thing is a cloth-covered tester, which looked as if the preacher had put up his sunshade to dry and left it there in about 1950, so that it has become a permanent fixture.

Nearby are the 1728 almshouses built for five people with 16 steps leading to three arches in the gable, an unusual piece of architecture.

St James, Lathom Chapel

Lathom is near Ormskirk and St James was built in 1500 to celebrate the victory at Bosworth, for Lord Stanley became Earl of Derby. This is a large chapel, used regularly, with windows dating from 1823 designed by the 21-year-old Hon. Mary Bootle-Wilbraham whose family lived in the rebuilt house during Napoleonic times.

In 1964, Ernest Gee restored the building, repainting the wagon roof and uncovering a Perpendicular door. The chancel screen and the eagle lectern, both older than the chapel, came from Burscough Priory after its dissolution.

Lathom is famous for its long defence by Lady Stanley, when her Royalist husband was away in the Isle of Man; she held out with a tiny garrison for three months. The Earl returned and rescued his family, but could not save the house from being destroyed. In 1651 he was captured at Worcester and executed at Bolton. The chapel was damaged but repaired so that only its history remains with the nearby vestries and almshouses.

Other churches to see in Lancashire:

St Peter, Heysham

Now part of Morecambe, Heysham still runs a ferry over to the Isle of Man. The church is Anglo-Saxon. The chancel arch has an Early Norman capital and rope mouldings. There is a Perpendicular screen, seventeeth-century font cover and, in the nave, a hogsback tombstone supposed to be of Viking origin. Nearby is St Patrick's Chapel, measuring 27½ft x 9ft, dating to the ninth century and with a doorway carved from one stone. Here it is believed St Patrick landed from Ireland. Next to the chapel are some unusual graves cut out of the rock.

St Peter, Far Sawrey

Quite a large chunk of Lancashire is in the Lake District, including Hill Top where Beatrix Potter lived and wrote her Peter Rabbit stories. Her church was at Far Sawrey; built in 1866, it is aisle-less, with a north-east tower and transepts. Pevsner calls it a 'decent, honest piece of work'.

LEICESTERSHIRE

A county that looks after its hedges and is proud of its churches. The County Council publish a useful leaflet *Framland Church Trail* obtainable from Melton Mowbray Tourist Information Centre. It doesn't include the smallest church at Drayton.

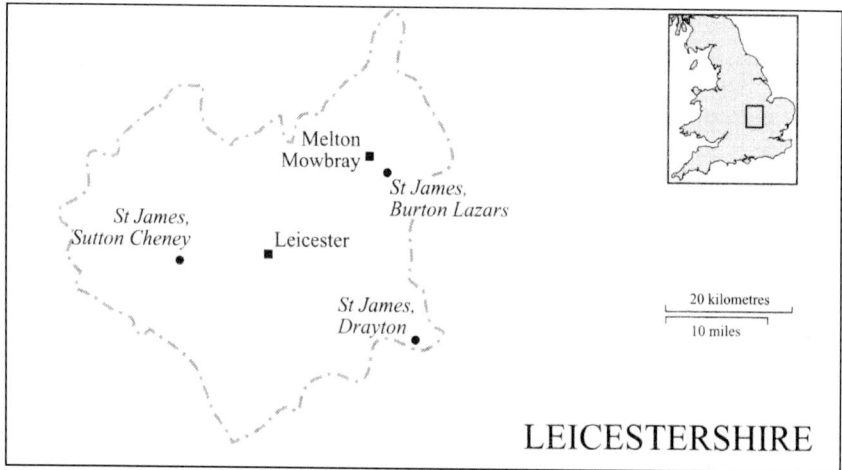

St James, Drayton

Drayton is a small village, more like a hamlet, on the Leicestershire–Rutland border. The villages have attractive yellow stone buildings hereabouts and Drayton is no exception. The tiny one-cell church of St James is in the middle of the green. There is a metal plate that tells us this was once a chapel of ease of Bringhurst parish, but ceased to be used for worship in the eighteenth century. It became a bakery – rather the reverse of what happened at St Michaels Chapel, Downside (see p.121). However, the Watsons of nearby Rockingham Castle restored it in 1878 and it is used every Sunday. It measures 24ft 4in x 14ft and has only 20 chairs, although extra ones are sometimes added. The key is obtainable from Brookside.

St James, Sutton Cheney

Standing on the side of the battlefield of Bosworth, St James' Church at Sutton Cheney is supposed to be where King Richard III came to say his prayers before the battle (August 1485). Inside the church, the Richard III Society have erected a brass plate with Richard's coat of arms and the words:

> RICHARD III
> King of England
> And those who fell
> At Bosworth Field
> Having kept Faith
>
> 22nd August 1485
> *Loyaulte me lie*

The church dates from the thirteenth century or earlier, but the north wall was rebuilt in 1826 and the box pews are eighteenth century. There was further work done in 1905 when the chancel was rebuilt. Now the bells are unsafe to ring and one bell, dated 1678, stands inside the south door. There are monuments with coats of arms to Sir William Roberts and Lord of the Manor, Geoffrey May. Around the church, look at the kneelers and you will see the shield of Sir Richard Ratcliffe, killed in the battle fighting for his king, the cat symbol of Sir William Catesby who was executed after the battle and the dog symbol of Viscount Lovel who escaped. Many years later, Lovel's house at Minster Lovell was being repaired when some

St James, Sutton Cheynell, now known as Sutton Cheney

workmen discovered a secret room. Inside was the body of Viscount Lovel – a mystery today, but to all accounts he died of starvation when his trusty servant failed to appear.

In springtime there are daffodils and Sutton Cheney is a cheerful place. It is a spot not to be missed. The symbol of a shell, representing St James, appears on the cover of the guidebook. Not far away in Warwickshire there are shells on the tower of Astley Church which overlooks the ruins of the former home of Lady Jane Grey. (The Landmark Trust have recently repaired this building).

The Melton Mowbray Church Trail

The Leicestershire County Council Tourist Department has set up the Framland Church Trail, which is based on Melton Mowbray, conveniently situated on the Leicester–Peterborough railway line. The 14 churches listed on their brochure are: St Mary, Melton Mowbray; St Mary the Virgin, Bottesford; St Michael and All Angels, Stapleford; St Botolph and St John the Baptist, Croxton Kerrial; St Mary the Virgin, Burrough on the Hill; Gaddesby St Luke (with its monument of Colonel Cheney on a dead horse), Eaton St Denys; St Mary Magdalene, Waltham on the Wolds; St Gulac, Branston; and finally St James, Burton Lazars. The last church, on the A6003 just south of Melton, is quite small. It dates from the twelfth and thirteenth centuries, and has a splendid roof with a strange bell tower that appears as if a miniature church had been built on the roof to hold the two bells. In the churchyard are graves to the two Counts Zborowski, father and son, motor racers. Luigi, the son, built the car used in the film *Chitty Chitty Bang Bang*. The name 'Burton Lazars' comes from the leper colony that used to be here. The St Mary and Lazars Hospital existed between 1160 and 1544. It is a church not to be missed, and is open on the first Sunday of the month, May to October from 2.30 to 5pm.

LINCOLNSHIRE

One of the largest counties and full of interesting churches. There are at least 700 of them and the county is divided into three parts: Lindsey, Kesteven and Holland. The Saxons divided these into sokes and wapentakes. Lindsey, between Lincoln and the Humber has most of the small churches, so I made Wragby my base. The late Henry Thorold has written about them in *Lincolnshire Churches Revisited,* reissued in 1993. He cites a signpost near Old Bolingbroke Castle which says 'To Mavis Enderby and Old Bolingbroke'. Underneath this is some graffiti which says 'A son, both doing well'.

The Lincolnshire Old Churches Trust recommended the first two of the following churches:

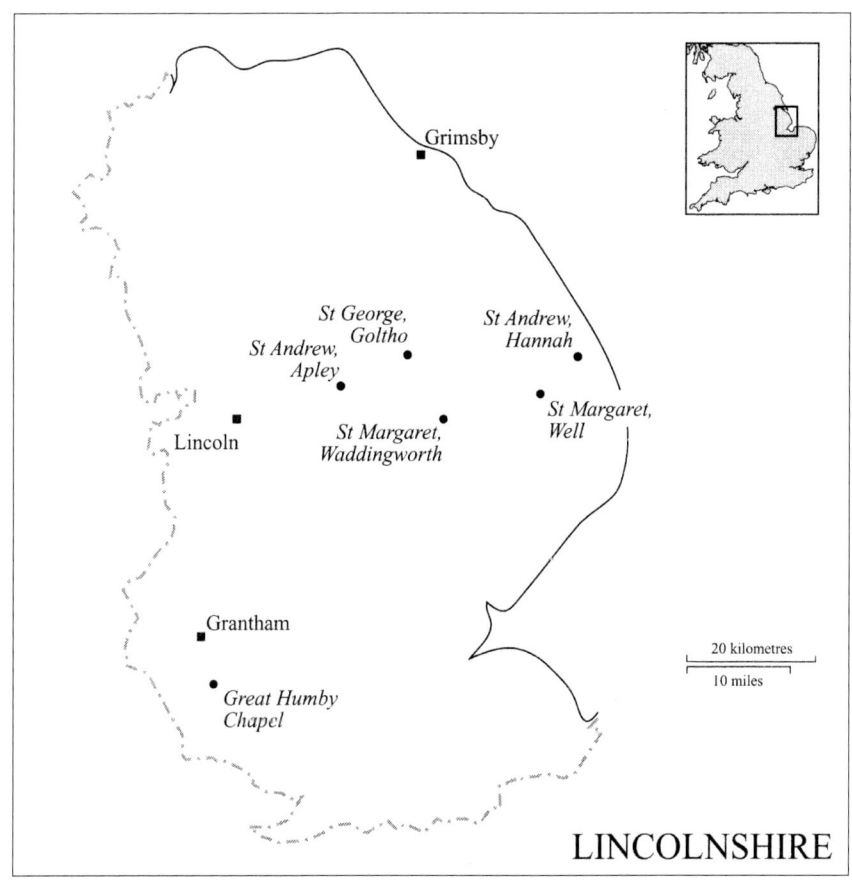

Great Humby Chapel

This measures 30ft x 15ft and stands alone in a field. It was the private chapel of Humby House, the home of the Brownlow family before they moved to Belton. The chapel we see is a 1754 rebuild minus one bay, but the earlier building was 1684. It has large mullioned three-light windows and a doorway with a blank keystone. The bell gable is incorporated into the end gable. Interior fittings date from 1876 and the restoration from 1980. It was restored and vested in the Lincolnshire Old Churches Trust in 1980 and is now used regularly. Humby is a few miles to the east of Grantham.

St George, Goltho

Goltho means where marigolds grow. Close to Wragby on a hill, the little brick church is all that remains of a medieval village. The nave is 18ft long and contains the monument to Thomas Grantham who died in the 1650s. The manor site was excavated by Guy Beresford in the 1980s, who found that the original church was much larger. It is thought that the first building might have been built of wood like St Andrew, Greensted. Goltho was regularly used until 1960, and is now in the care of the Churches Conservation Trust. Goltho was badly burnt in 2012 and the Trust have not yet decided whether to repair it. Goltho also appeared in the wedding of *Tom Jones*, the film which reappears on television from time to time.

St Margaret, Waddingworth

This is a happier story. A rather ordinary little church built of brick, oolite and greenstone sits in the middle of a farmyard (the farmer keeps the key) which until the 1980s was redundant. Waddingworth is a hamlet close to Horncastle and has a stone near the church which it claims to be the centre of England. Inside the little church is a monument to Edward Dymoke, who was champion of England and died in 1729. In 1973, Fred Ainstrup, organ builder, purchased St Margaret's which had been de-consecrated three years before. Until 1998, it was used as an organ store but then Fred's colleague, Chris Hind, formed a committee to restore it. A second-hand organ was installed with carpets and chairs. Gutters and lead work were replaced. Church commissioners had to be informed and a change of use authorised by East Lindsey District Council. Finally, on Harvest Festival 1999, the church re-opened with 60 people attending. Since then the Revd Janet Platt runs an occasional service with candles for lighting.

The late Henry Thorold tells how the bells fell from the belfry in 1914 and again in 1939 with disastrous results to world affairs. Just as the Gulf War erupted, it was found the single bell was hanging from one weak bracket so World War III may have been prevented by the prompt repair of both brackets. St Margaret's is well worth a visit.

Other small churches to see in Lincolnshire:

St Andrew, Apley

This is a mortuary chapel not far from Wragby which at the moment is being used as a church. It dates from 1871 and is made of red brick.

St Andrew, Hannah

An eighteenth-century greenstone church with a west porch dating from 1753 and not far from the sea between Alford and Sutton, St Andrew's Church has a Georgian interior with a two-decker pulpit, Georgian altar rails, chandelier, marble font with wooden cover and curved altar rails. It should not be missed.

St Margaret, Well

This is an unusual little Palladian church built by James Bateman, brother of Lord Bateman of Shobdon in Herefordshire, in 1733. From the outside looks more like a summerhouse than a church, but inside it is much larger. The bellcote was replaced in 1970. The pews face inwards like a chapel and there is a three-decker pulpit in the middle of the south wall with tester. There is a reredos and commandment boards. Well is a mile south of Alford and the key to the church can be found at the estate office on the farm.

LONDON

To write an introduction to London and its churches is not easy. However I have detached Middlesex, which I think is a separate county architecturally and in the minds of those who live there, and I have included the Tower to cover the City, where the churches can best be seen on foot. I have also included Old St Pancras, which is on an island of calm in a sea of rebuilding and is only a few steps from the railway station.

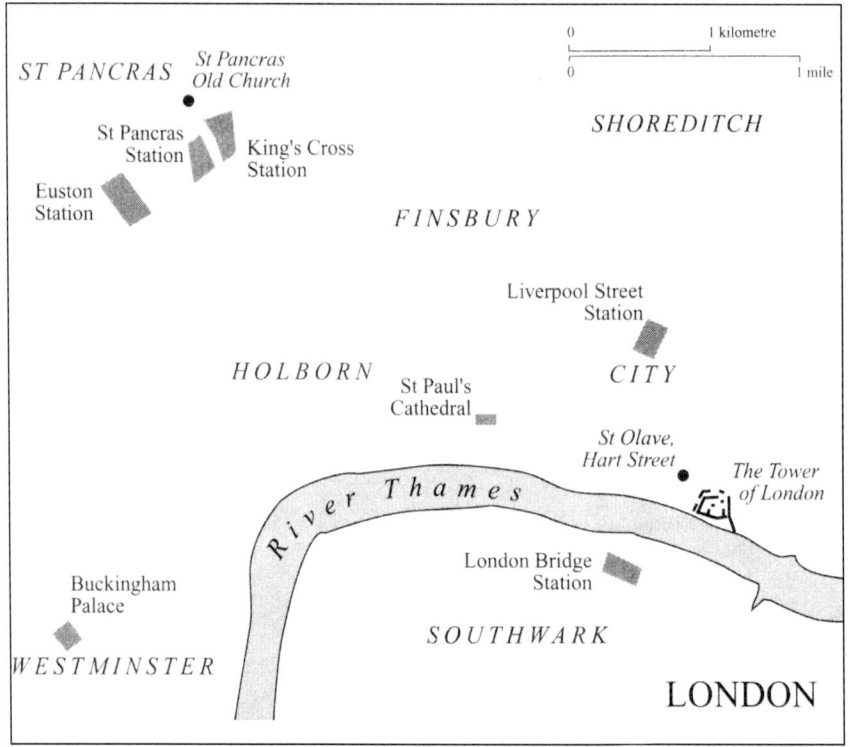

THE TOWER

St Peter ad Vincula, Chapel Royal

This was once a parish church but was incorporated into the Tower when the latter was enlarged by Henry III. *Ad vincula* means 'in chains'; an appropriate dedication when we think of prisoners, but it is St Peter who was in chains and the name predates the use of the Tower as a prison.

From the outside, St Peter looks tiny, but inside it has two bays, a chancel and two Spanish chestnut roofs. It is the parish church of those 40 Yeoman Warders and their families. There is a stone in the chancel floor recalling the unfortunate people executed at the Tower, namely:

Lord Guilford Dudley	1554
Lady Jane Grey	1554
Henry Grey	1554
Thomas Howard, Duke of Northumberland	1572
Earl of Arundel	1595
Robert Devereux, Earl of Essex	1601
Sir Thomas Overbury (Murdered in the Tower)	1613

The chapel was built after the execution of Anne Boleyn and Catherine Howard which is presumably why they aren't on the chancel floor stone.

By the door are the three coffin plates, in lead, of the three Jacobite lords executed after the 1745 rebellion. The last to be executed, Simon Fraser, Lord Lovat, was a large fat man of 80 years. The body buried here, according to tradition, is that of a young thin man and the actual body of Lovat was taken back to Scotland for a family grave.

There are monuments on the wall to famous Field Marshals who were Governors here – Wellington, Alexander, Wavell and others. The very fine organ comes from the Palace of Westminster, has carvings by Gibbons and dates from 1699. The two monuments that take up space are not of great importance. One is to Sir Richard Cholmondley and his wife. He was Lieutenant Governor, but fell out of favour, so is not buried here. During the Civil War, the Parliamentarians held the Tower and the outgoing chaplain hid the font inside a tomb. John Holland's tomb has been moved here from St Katherine's Church, Regents Park. It seems Holland introduced the rack to the Tower and it was something our Warder guide, who had the key in his belt, was proud of and it seemed to go down well with tourists.

Chapel of St John the Evangelist

This is on the first floor of the White Tower. It dates from Early Norman times and has a tunnel-vaulted nave and gallery. Pevsner shows a photograph of it next to St Bartholomew, Smithfield which is later and more elaborate. There is seating for 50, mostly in the nave and on the side walls. The chapel was used by Queen Mary for her proxy wedding to Philip of Spain. Here Lady Jane Grey said her prayers before being led to the scaffold at the age of 16. Henry VII's wife, Elizabeth of York, who died in childbirth, lay in state here in 1503. The sovereign used the chapel for private services and it was used by the Tower Choir when they appeared on *Songs of Praise*.

Edward's Oratory

The two chapels are really too large for the purposes of this book, but the Oratory of King Edward I is too small. It is to be found in the turret of St Thomas' Tower, which would have overlooked the river in King Edward's day. It seems Edward had a narrow escape when playing chess. He moved to a different chair and his former chair was crushed when a stone fell down from the ceiling. He attributed his escape to the Virgin Mary and her Walsingham shrine. Henceforward, he became superstitious and a great believer in fate.

Bell Tower Chapel

The Bell Tower on the corner of Mint Street and Water Lane is, apart from the White Tower, the oldest in the Tower (1190). It has been built in two stages, firstly with polygonal sides then a round tower above. The bell itself is in a wooden belfry and dates from 1651, but an earlier bell there was used for curfew. This is where Sir Thomas More was imprisoned by Henry VIII for refusing to accept the King as Head of the Church. His picture hangs inside the Tower. The Roman Catholics use it for a mass at least twice a year. The arrow loop in the main room makes a cross, appropriate for a prison room and also for an occasional chapel.

LONDON'S SMALLEST CHURCH

A few years ago, this was either St Anne, Abbey Orchard Street (RC), demolished to make a block of flats, or St Ethelburga in Bishopsgate. The latter was destroyed by the IRA in 1993 and it has since been rebuilt as a Centre for Peace and Reconciliation.

The current favourite for the smallest church, big by out-of-town standards, is St Olave's, Hart Street. This was originally a fifteenth-century church, but was destroyed in the Blitz and restored in the 1950s by E.B. Glanfield. The pulpit comes from St Benet, Gracechurch Street, and some of the other fittings were rescued, including two of the metal sword rests. It is famous for the memorial of Mrs Pepys (1669), according to Pevsner 'Admonishing (permanently) her wayward husband'. He has a small Victorian monument of 1884 with a portrait roundel.

St Pancras, London, in its pre-railway appearance

N.B. Bridget Cherry, who edits the Pevsner books, has pointed out to me that St Ethelburga's is indeed the smallest church in the City of London, but has a nave of 55¼ft long and is only open as a select conference centre. Before its nineteenth-century renovations, the smallest church was St Pancras Old Church (not to be confused with the Greek Revival building in Upper Woburn Place) in Pancras Road. It is one of the oldest London churches – the guide says it was first built in AD 313 or 314. In 1840, the church was enlarged, as it was again after being damaged in the Blitz. The drawing shows the original church and cemetery when St Pancras had a footpath and stile and the railways were not yet in the area.

Inside is the monument to William Platt, moved from Highgate Chapel. He was a London brewer and related to Richard, founder (1597) of Aldenham School. There is also a sixth-century altar stone marked with five consecration crosses, which are, it is thought, only found at one other place – on the tomb of Ethne, mother of St Columba who died in AD 597.

MIDDLESEX

Another of John Betjeman's favourite counties and he says 'Looking for Middlesex is even more fun than looking for Middlesex churches'. He would not be pleased to know that the county doesn't officially exist, but pleased to know it is included here and that those who live there still expect you to put 'Mddx' on their addresses.

The diocese recommends the smallest church, which is well worth a visit.

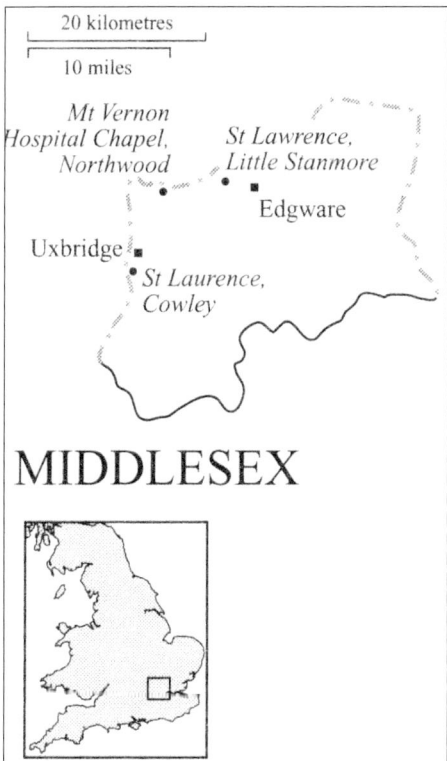

St Laurence, Cowley

This little flint church is found at the end of Station Road and is on a bus route from Uxbridge Station. The key is with the Vicar next door and the building dates from 1780. There is an unusual two-storey gallery and the roof has a strange arched king-post supporting beam which looks as if someone had put up a couple of medieval bed heads to support the roof.

In the well-used churchyard is the grave of William Dodd, a king's chaplain born in 1729. He became tutor to the 5th Earl of Chesterfield and had a reputation for fine sermons. However, he tried to bribe the wife of the Lord Chancellor to obtain the rectorship of fashionable St George's, Hanover Square, was lampooned in the press, struck off the list of chaplains and attempted to forge Lord Chesterfield's signature on a bond for £4,200. He was caught and sentenced to be hanged at Tyburn. One of Dodd's gambling friends attempted to bribe the gaoler but, alas, in 1777 Dodd was hanged. Also in the graveyard is the tomb of Barton Booth, an eighteenth-century actor and apparently without a rival as Hamlet's ghost.

Other small churches to see in Middlesex:

St Lawrence, Little Stanmore – the Chandos Mausoleum

This is a remarkable Baroque building attached to the church. It was built by Marlborough's pay-master general, Lord Chandos, in 1735. The architect was James Gibbs and the statue of the Duke dressed as a Roman is by Andrew Carpentier, although some consider it to be by Grinling Gibbons. The chapel is near to Canons Park tube station and is open on Sundays between 3-5pm (summer) and 2-4pm (winter).

Mt Vernon Hospital Chapel, Northwood

Situated on a hill with large windows and Voysey-like buttresses, the chapel dates from 1904 and was built by F.L. Wheeler in the Art Nouveau style. It has a small west bell tower. Today it is divided and only used for a service on St Luke's day (18 October). The other part is a hospital library.

The chapel was opened in September 1904 by Princess Christian and her cavalry bodyguard. The following year it was dedicated by the Bishop of Islington. In 1985 it was given a full-time chaplain and today it is used mostly as a library and conference centre and for the occasional service. To see it, permission must obtained from the hospital.

NORFOLK

Norfolk is full of flint churches, mostly too large for this book. There are nine small churches, one of which has been recommended by the Round Tower Society.

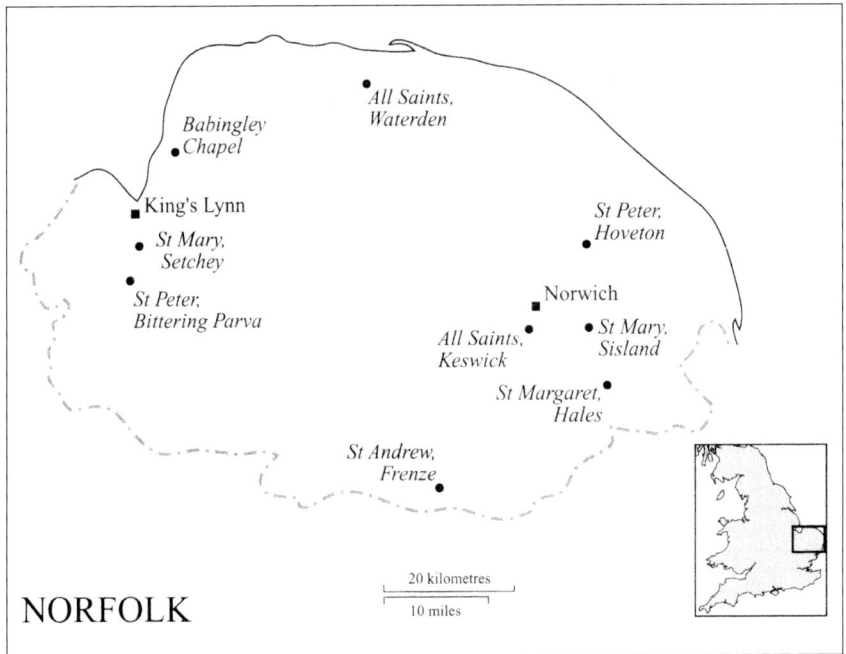

St Peter, Hoveton

Tucked away near Wroxham, the centre for cruising in the Broads, St Peter's, Hoveton is a surprise. For a start, it is built entirely of brick and secondly it dates from 1624, an unusual age for a small church. The outside was once rendered and painted white. Inside, and you need to be a rugby player to open the door, preferably in the scrum, it was arranged as a college chapel, but the present pews were put in there by H.J. Green in 1885. There is a wooden carving of the Royal Arms of Charles II, a twentieth-century font and a fine series of hatchments on the wall – those with scallop shells belong to the Negus family and those with grapes to the Aufrere family. There is a bell dating from 1624 and a chalice (1803) and paten (1710) which were presented to Sco Ruston Church (now derelict) by the Revd Mack in 1844.

The smallest church in Norfolk has been the subject of some correspondence in the local newspaper and, apart from Hoveton, there is a round tower church near Norwich on a hill which may qualify. This is:

All Saints, Keswick

Situated quite close to the University of East Anglia, Keswick Church stands alone on a small hill. Inside, it has a 1922 Morris window, and the original west wall, so the feeling is a bit cramped.

Built from the ruins of an old Saxon church, this is the smallest round tower church. It has a new apsidal chancel and is only 14ft x 18ft in the nave. The tower with its brick bell openings was restored in 1893 and the church rebuilt five years later. The bell has *Josephus Carter Me Fecit 1609* on it and the sound must ring loudly across the valley, but as there are very few houses around, one wonders where the congregation comes from.

There are small angels on the wall beams and the village postmistress has a small memorial in the vestry. This church is tucked away down a very bumpy lane and the key is obtainable from Mill Lane Cottage.

Other small churches in Norfolk:

Babingley Chapel

This is a thatch-roofed tin chapel that belongs to the Orthodox Church of Alexandria. It is used regularly and stands close to where St Felix landed when bringing Christianity to East Anglia.

St Peter, Bittering Parva

A long single roof church not far from Dereham, this is mostly an Early English fifteenth-century construction with a west gable of the seventeenth century. There is a fine 1925 east lancet window of the Crucifixion by Lydall Armitage. Bittering is one of Bishop Nott's favourite small churches in Norfolk. It is well looked after and has a monthly service.

St Andrew, Frenze

Tucked away down a farm lane to Diss, Frenze is just a nave with a bell-turret. It was restored in 1900, but today is looked after by the Churches Conservation Trust. It is built of flint and rubble, and has a gabled brick porch. This is Tudor brick as one Margaret James left a cow in her will of 1521 for this rebuilding. The inside has Jacobean furniture, but the main point of interest is the large number of brasses to the Blenerhaysset family from the nearby Hall. They are mostly fifteenth and sixteenth century and Mary Bacon, who was a daughter of the family, spells her name Blenerhaiset just to be different. This is a church that is worth discovering.

St Margaret, Hales

A thatched church with a round tower that is looked after by the Churches Conservation Trust, Hales is close to Lodden. It has an apsidal chancel and the nave length is 43ft 4in. The screen is painted red and green, the organ case dates from 1815 and there is a fourteenth-century oil painting of angels blowing the trumpet. There are no pews or evidence of any and it is thought the church originally had chairs or removable benches.

St Mary, Setchey

A few miles south of Kings Lynn, St Mary's Church was built in 1844, a three-bay nave and small chancel with a west doorway. This church has now become a private house although the churchyard is still being used for burials.

St Mary, Sisland

St Mary's Church was built in 1761 on the site of an earlier church that had been struck by lightning. The nave and chancel are of brick and the building was once whitewashed and thatched. There is a west gallery on iron rods, a fifteenth-century font and a tri-partite chancel arch. The font is decorated with lions and there is a seventeenth-century font cover. Sisland is between Norwich and Lodden.

All Saints, Waterden

South of Burnham Market, this is an interesting church which, from the outside, looks like two chapels joined together. It has Norman south and north doorways, and some rather out-of-place seventeenth-century transom windows. There are upper windows which look Saxon, a fourteenth-century font and box pews. There is a service here in the summer, once a month. Waterden has a deserted village site.

NORTHAMPTONSHIRE

Northamptonshire has mostly tall churches with broached spires and there are not many small churches.

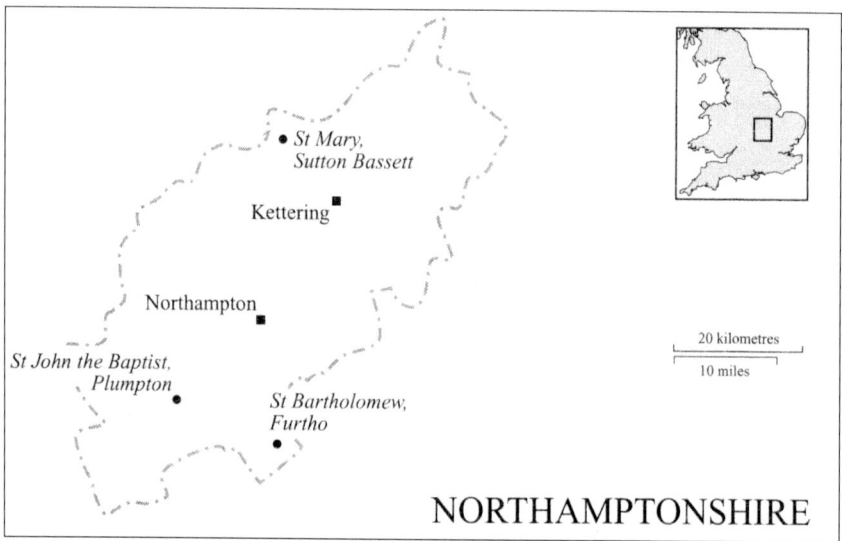

St John the Baptist, Plumpton

A few miles north of Brackley there is a church in a small hamlet, Plumpton St John, that has a 30ft nave and a small font 6ft from the west end. It is mostly of 1822 date and, when I called in March, the Christmas decorations were still there. Outside it looks a bit derelict and in need of care. It has box pews, benches and commandment boards. The chancel has at one time been painted. The organ was presented in 1973 by the Second Baron Astor of Hever in memory of his parents who worshipped here between 1920 and 1962.

The only interesting history of the hamlet is that it used to belong to two heiresses and one of them was married to Baron de Caux. He persuaded her to sell out to the other on condition that 50 marks were donated to Hayle Abbey and a further 50 to the building of a new Westminster Abbey church. Presumably this she did and Plumpton contributed to the building of one of our most famous churches. The living is with Jesus College, Oxford and the key is kept in the house next door.

Other small churches in Northamptonshire:

St Bartholomew, Furtho

Some 10 miles south of Northampton off the A508, Furtho is a deserted village. The church dates mostly from 1620 and is looked after by the Churches Conservation Trust. It has wooden two- and three-light windows and the chancel, which is fourteenth century, has a roof higher than the nave.

St Mary, Sutton Bassett

On the Leicestershire border, St Mary's Church seems to be in the middle of the village close to the road. It has nave, chancel and bellcote, and is mostly Norman. There is a tympanum with squares and lozenge pattern decoration, known as diapering.

NORTHUMBERLAND

England's most northerly county again has mostly large churches and the two recommended by the Diocesan office in Newcastle are too large. Instead, with help from Geoff Briggs, I have recommended the following small churches.

St Francis of Assisi, Byrness

Byrness is the first settlement you come to on the A68 after coming down from Scotland. The church stands by the road and the key can be found in the garage shop nearby. It was built by the Revd Dutems, Vicar of Elsdon in 1796 and the chancel Victorianised in 1884. It is a simple stone building with a round-headed south doorway and windows.

1 (Above left) St Michael, Farndish, Bedfordshire © *Author*

2 (Above) St Thomas, East Shefford, Berkshire © *Author*

3 (Left) All Saints, Little Kimble, Buckinghamshire © *Author*

4 Guyhirn Chapel, Cambridgeshire © *Author*

5 Our Lady & St Anne, Widemouth Bay, Cornwall © *Author*

6 St Edith, Shocklach, Cheshire © *B. Lowry*

7 St Mary, Honeychurch, Devon © *Harland Walshaw*

8 (Above) St Bega, Bassenthwaite, Cumbria © *Harland Walshaw*

9 (Left) St Martin, Wareham, Dorset © *J. Catling Allen*

10 St Michael de Rupe, Brentor, Devon © *Harland Walshaw*

11 St Peter's Chapel, Bradwell-Juxta-Mare, Essex © *J. Catling Allen*

12 St John, Elkstone, Gloucestershire © *Author*

13 St Mary, Syde, Gloucestershire © *Author*

14 St Hubert, Idsworth, Hampshire © *Harland Walshaw*

15 Fleur Kelly's millennium fresco at St Hubert, Idsworth © *Author*

16 St John, Little Gidding, Huntingdonshire © *Peter Burton & Harland Walshaw*

17 St Margaret, St Margarets, Herefordshire © *Author*

18 Sixteenth-century screen at St Margaret, St Margarets © *Author*

19 St Margaret, Waddingworth, Lincolnshire © *Author*

20 (Left) St Lawrence, Cowley, Middlesex © *Author*

21 (Below) Chapel of St John the Evangelist, Tower of London © *Crown Copyright, Historic Royal Palaces*

22 All Saints, Keswick, Norfolk
© *Author*

23 St Andrew, Sookholme, Nottinghamshire © *Author*

24 (Left) St Giles, Carburton, Nottinghamshire – naval type interior
© *Author*

25 (Below) St Oswald, Widford, Oxfordshire
© *Author*

26 St Beuno, Culbone, Somerset © *Mick Sharp*

27 St Peter, Melverley, Shropshire. The Vrynwy in flood © *B. Lowry*

28 St Peter, Melverley, interior © *B. Lowry*

29 Interior of Langely Chapel, Shropshire © *B. Lowry*

30 St Michael, Up Marden, Sussex © *Harland Walshaw*

31 Church of the Good Shepherd, Lullington, Sussex © *J. Catling Allen*

32 St Michael, Hanley Childe, Worcestershire © *Author*

33 Kempe Window at St. Leonard, Chapel-le-Dale, W. Yorkshire © *Author*

The south window commemorates those who died in the construction of Catcleugh Reservoir (1903) and shows a narrow gauge steam railway. There were women, children and men who died due to existing in the shanty town with insufficient food and shelter. The west side drops down to the extensive churchyard where there are some interesting graves, one with a skull and crossbones.

The 'village' nearby was built in the 1950s for Forestry Commission workers by Dr Thomas Sharp. Why didn't he include the church in his plan? It is easier to reach from the garage.

St Cuthbert, Haydon (Old Church)

Not to be confused with St Cuthbert in Haydon Bridge which is a large church in town (with an interesting 1983 window to St Cuthbert) the little church of Old Haydon is well hidden in a walled enclosure down a lane at the top of the hill. Before finding it you have to collect the key from Clarke's Newsagents. It has a short nave, 18ft 3in, a side chapel with a delightful window showing St Simeon and a twelfth-century chancel. The east end has three slit windows showing saints with unusual round-faced pilasters between them. There is a monument to a local worthy who captained a regiment in 1745 in a time of troubles with the Jacobites.

The churchyard must be a problem to keep tidy and the avenue of trees from the road makes it not an easy church to get to; it is difficult to find space for a car, so for those energetic enough you have to leave it in the town and walk up the steep hill.

St Cuthbert is one of a team of churches, another of which is the wooden St Aidan's, Fourstones (1892) which is painted green. It was firmly locked but still in business.

Other small churches to see in Northumberland:

Holy Trinity, Old Bewick

Holy Trinity is a small church with nave and apsidal chancel about half a mile from the village. It is mostly Norman and very impressive inside. The arch of the chancel is followed by a Norman arch of the squared-off apse. Restored in 1866, the church has star and cable decoration, and the north capital has grotesque heads, teeth and pointed cat-like ears.

St Aidan, Thockrington

St Aidan is another Norman church in a remote place 7 miles west of Belsay. Two Norman windows remain and inside there are two plain twelfth-century arches with a round tunnel vault between them. The chancel is propped up by two large stepped corner buttresses, as the church appears to be falling downhill. There is a large twin bell-turret and in the graveyard is the tomb of Lord Beveridge, famous for his report implementing our social services of 1942. He was also the mastermind behind food rationing during the Second World War and after.

NOTTINGHAMSHIRE

This is Robin Hood country, lots of trees and parks amidst the old coal mines. The Southwell Diocese recommended four churches, two of which are redundant and one of which was locked when I called. The smallest is to be found at Carburton.

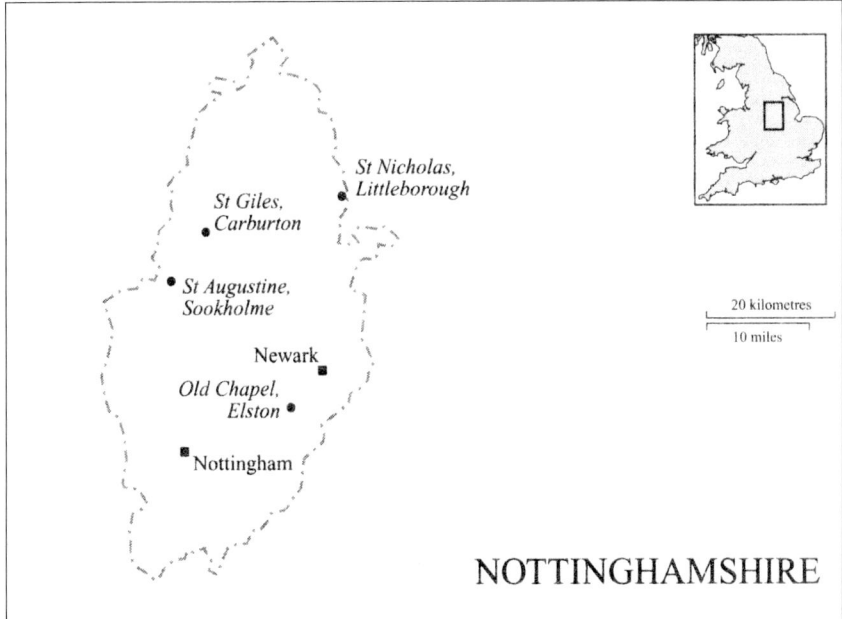

St Giles, Carburton

This little church, covered in concrete with a tank-like bell tower, is situated near the entrance to Clumber Park (National Trust) and used to be larger. The Norman building has a south aisle, removed by 1748, so the south wall now looks strange, with the windows outlined as if there was a piece missing. Inside, and the south door is usually open, the seating is painted battleship grey – the whole church would look at home on a naval base at Scapa Flow or Rosyth – and the nave measures 27½ft.

There is a small brass next to the altar in memory of John Mazine, Armour Bearer of the Royal Stable and one of the Duke of Nottingham's cavalry at Marston Moor who died in 1677. There is a west window dated to 1938 and three original windows in the chancel.

Other churches to see in Nottinghamshire:

Chapel (no dedication), Elstone

Looked after by the Churches Conservation Trust, this little chapel stands in a field of horses and one has to walk carefully to see it. There is a west gallery, hat pegs on the wall, box pews, a squire's pew, Jacobean pulpit and reader's desk, all about 1820 or older.

St Nicholas, Littleborough

This is another aisle-less Norman church with a lot of herringbone masonry close to the Trent, where the Lincoln–Doncaster road was forded. Inside, the arch profile to the chancel is out of keeping with the rest of the interior.

St Augustine, Sookholme

St Augustine's is close to a farm, but before visiting it, it is necessary to visit Church Warsop vicarage (opposite the church there) to collect the key. It is more of a chapel than a church, c.1100, and like Carburton has three east windows, two below and one above in the centre. There are other decorated windows, a low sedilia – a stone seat with low arms – and a couple of ancient beams.

OXFORDSHIRE

The small churches of Oxfordshire tend to be family chapels, but there is a great variety in the county. The industrial north, the limestone town and the chalky south end all produce different building materials. The smallest church in the county and, according to its guidebook, the sixth smallest in England is at Yelford.

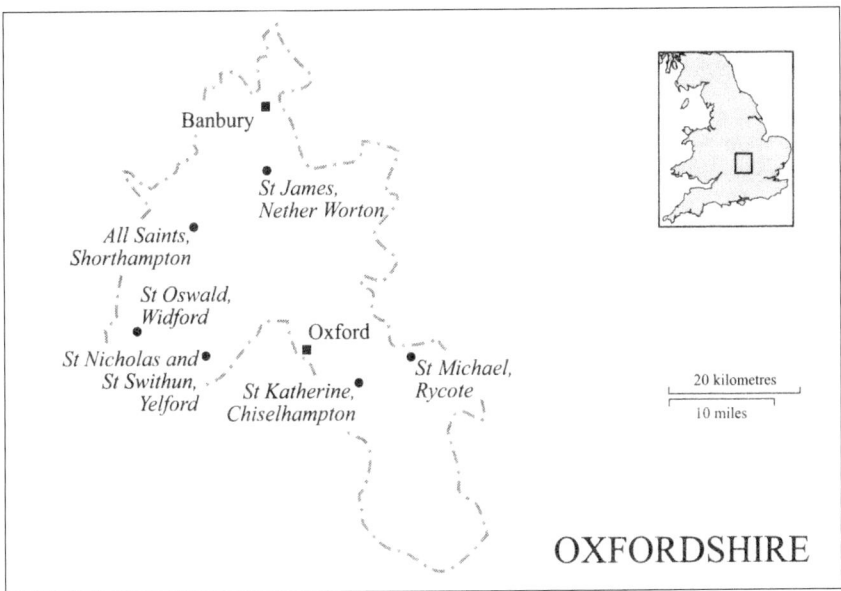

St Nicholas & St Swithun, Yelford

To find this village, take the A420 Swindon–Oxford road and turn off at the A415 junction near Fyfield. After Standlake there is a long narrow road over a hill that drops down into the hamlet of Yelford. The church is easy to miss and there is no easy place to park. There is a fifteenth-century black and white wooden-framed manor house nearby which would be more at home in Lavenham or in Cheshire.

The church has a short nave 32ft 3in x 16ft 3in and a small chancel 20ft x 12ft 3in. The living was in the hands of Veronica Babington Smith, whose sister-in-law Constance was the WAAF officer famous for discovering the photograph of Peenemunde during the Second World War. Another member of the family worked under cover in Northern Ireland. Today the manor belongs to a Mr Rosewall who was opening the garden to the public on the day we called.

Most of the church dates from 1500, but the bellcote is Victorian. There is a mass-dial inside and to the right of the door. The quatrefoil screen, octagonal font and piscine are all original, but the pews date from 1873 and the church was re-roofed in 1955 and a new lectern made. Ten years later the pulpit was installed. The French organ was inserted in 1993. There is no burial ground here as the land is so low-lying. Maybe they had the same problem as the gravediggers of Burrowbridge, Somerset, who kept having to re-bury one particular coffin that floated to the top in floods. This is a church and manor house worth travelling miles to see.

There are several small churches in Oxfordshire, a county which gained much ground from Berkshire in the county reshuffle in the 1970s. Richard Lethbridge has recommended three of the five churches I have included, but of the other two, one he scarcely mentions and the other he excludes altogether. This one is:

St Katherine, Chiselhampton

A Georgian gem standing by the main road to Cowley (B480). The bell turret and royal blue clock stand at the west end with twin scroll pediments flanked by urns at the corners. The date is 1762 and the architect is supposed to be Sam Dowbiggin of London. The porcelain dealer who built the church, Charles Peers, chose the dedication after the name of his wife. Inside there are numerous Peers monuments, including one to Charles put there by Tryphena, his third surviving wife. There is also a more modern monument to Sir Charles Reed Peers, Surveyor of Fabric at Westminster Abbey, who died in 1953. There is a fine reredos (see Rycote), a Jacobean pulpit (?from the old church), west gallery, box pews and clerk's desk with a reading desk. The chandeliers are Victorian and each pew has a little reading electric light, for this was the parish church until 1977 when it was handed over to the Churches Conservation Trust. The key (from next door) goes in upside down and turns the wrong way – handy for Australian tourists!

St James, Nether Worton

Three miles from Bloxham in the Tew Valley, this little church is easily missed. From outside, this church blends into its surrounding cottages so well that only the tower, in which there is the main entrance, and the windows give it away. There is a tower attached to a schoolroom and schoolteacher's cottage and the tower (1630) forms the porch. Inside, there is a 30ft nave, but two aisles so the church is nearly square. The nave arcades are Decorated, but much Early English work is evident on the aisle east walls. There is an unusual Victorian wall drawing in a frame of Christ bearing the cross. It needs special lighting to see it clearly. There is a sad monument to two of the Shuster family from the manor house, one killed in each of the World Wars, and a grand monument to William Wilson (1821) by Westmacott.

All Saints, Shorthampton. *Courtesy of Susan Woolley*

All Saints, Shorthampton

This church is near Charlbury off the Bloxham–Burford road and stands next to a house. Pevsner calls it 'small and humble'. It seems well-loved, unlike Nether Worton, and all the brass was gleaming. Originally Norman, it has been given a widened nave so that a large squint has had to be built for those in the aisle to see the altar. Box pews, a two-decker pulpit and some not easily identifiable wall paintings complete the picture. On the east of the door is St Eloi, a blacksmith, who is supposed to have shod a horse by removing one of its legs and then replacing it afterwards. This little church once had a west gallery and an outside door and stair to get to it. Susan Woolley's drawing shows the unusual roof and bell tower.

St Oswald, Widford

Wellington boots are required to see this church. Take the narrow lane from Fulbrook towards Swinbrook and look out for the stile and footpath leading down to Widford (population 11). In fact, when we reached Swinbrook there was a cricket match in progress, which may have accounted for the missing 11 from Widford. The church is on the dry side of a large bog and the entrance is round the south side. All was very spick and span with lots of notices not to bring in the mud. It is a thirteenth-century building which was been built by monks on the spot where St Oswald's body is supposed to have rested. He was Bishop of Worcester and a Benedictine monk, so may have died while visiting one of his outlying monasteries.

There is a nave of 24½ft, some nineteenth-century box pews, a set of strange flat communion rail balusters and some fragmentary wall paintings, one of which depicts kings on the north wall living and dead. Outside in the immaculately kept churchyard is an impressive sword tomb to John Lawrence of Buxton. There are services in summer on the third Sunday in the month at 6pm using the Book of Common Prayer.

St Michael, Rycote

Just outside Thame on the road to Wallingford stood Rycote House until it was pulled down in 1800 (although part of it is being rebuilt now). Rycote Chapel, which dates from 1449, is a mid-fifteenth century chantry chapel with some amazing woodwork inside. It was built by the Quatremaine family and has two elaborate family pews. The northern one has a minstrel placement on its roof with elaborately carved sides. The other gallery has a canopy roof, originally painted blue and silver and supposedly built for the visit of Charles I (1625). On the floor there are several lozenge memorial stones and on the wall a memorial to Alfred George Hamersley who lived at Rycote from 1911 to 1929 and preserved the chapel. This memorial is by Eric Gill. The barrel ceiling and the wagon roof complete the picture. Outside is an enormous yew tree, said to have been planted to commemorate King Stephen's coronation in 1135. Rycote is open Friday–Sunday and Bank Holidays, 2-6pm. There is a small admission charge.

Finally, although too large to include, visitors to Oxfordshire should see the late Norman church of St Mary the Virgin, Iffley, which has some splendid zigzag carving and a Piper window commemorating the artist (1995).

RUTLAND

Rutland is hunting country and full of large houses, small towns and large churches.

St Botolph, Wardley

This is, according to the Rural Dean, the smallest active church in the smallest county. It is tucked away near Uppingham down a cul-de-sac off the A416. The fourteenth-century tower and broach spire loom up on the left and the church looks much larger outside than it is inside. It has a doorway of 1175, the north door is blocked and much was restored in 1871. There used to be 'much blue paintwork' according to Pevsner, but this is not so obvious now. The organ has three barrels, each with 10 tunes and was made by T. Bates of Ludgate Hill, London, in the Victorian era.

There is an undecorated octagonal font and in the chancel a panel with the Sherard arms records the re-roofing of 1640. The monuments are mostly to the Brudenell family (Lord Cardigan of the Charge of the Light Brigade fame was a Brudenell), but there is a nice tablet to John Walker who died in 1859 and his wife Elizabeth who lived on until 1902.

During the Civil War the rector here, John Allington, carried on with the Laudian prayer book until at least 1655 when someone noticed this and he got into trouble.

Other small Rutland churches worth visiting:

St Peter & St Paul, Tickencote

Hidden away down a side road off the A1, St Peter and St Paul is famous for its Norman chancel arch with four orders and semi-circular responds. The chancel itself is vaulted, all dating from about 1160. The stained glass of 1929 by Nicholson fits in well, so too the square font. Tickencote has to be visited more than once to take it all in – a truly remarkable church.

St Mary Magdalene, Tixover

This is a church set in a field with a large Norman west tower, although the rest of the church is later. There is a porch, short nave (less than 30ft), two aisles and a long chancel with two spaced-out square-headed windows on each side. There are some stone bench tables along the north and south walls, one shortened on the south to take Roger Dale's monument of 1623 with his wife and two daughters. In 1984 Tixover was used in the filming of *Jane Eyre*.

SHROPSHIRE

The smallest church in this county is also the hardest to find. It stands below the mass of Brown Clee – Shropshire is full of large hills which turn white in the snow and stay white for some time – in a deserted village. I have also included the black and white church of Melverley near the Severn and the Welsh border, and Langley Chapel near Acton Burnell.

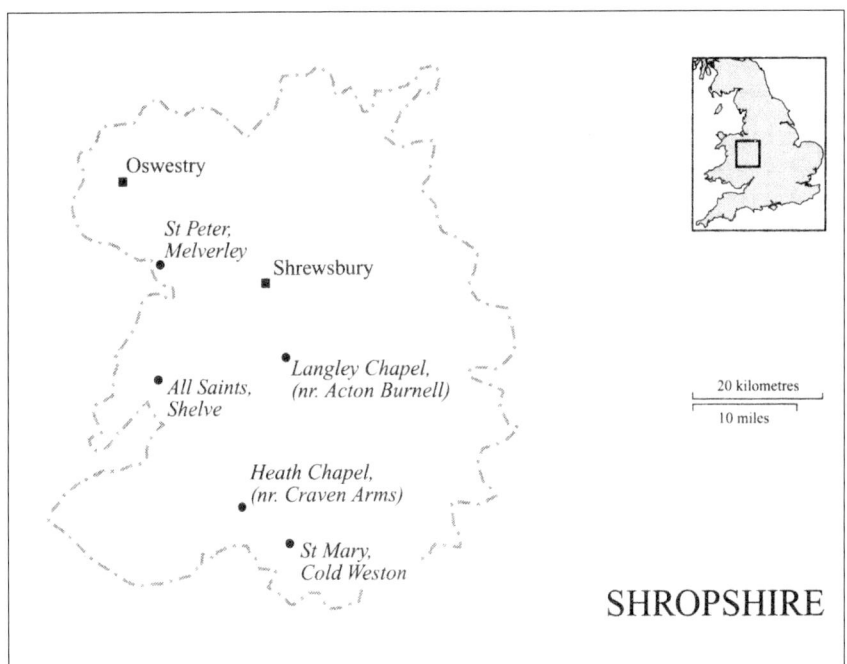

Heath Chapel

This is not strictly a chapel but a small Norman church with a graveyard nearby. We arrived on 13 August and there was a notice inside saying the next service was on Sunday, 11 August. We were two days late. This is not surprising, as to find Heath you take the A49 to the Craven Arms where you turn off on the B4368 to Diddlesbury, then you turn right through Peaton and Bouldon until you reach Upper Heath Farm, where the large key is in a box on the wall. Retrace your route by 300 yards and the church is in the field to the right of the road. Inside there are box pews, remains of a wall painting and a brass to the Revd Algernon Oldham, Archdeacon of Ludlow who restored the building in 1898 and preached his last sermon here in October 1912. Heath is a classic Norman church, untouched even by Algernon. It has a 29ft x 16ft nave and approximately 17½ft x 13ft chancel, although the angles are not square. The roof beams rest on wall posts that in some places have come adrift from the walls. The font looks as if it was dumped down by the builders and left. On it is the sad little face of a devil.

Heath is worth finding. Perhaps next time we come it will coincide with the August service.

St Peter, Melverley

This is a black and white church off the A458 and B4393 several miles west of Shrewsbury. The churchyard butts onto a cliff above the River Vyrnwy, a tributary of the Severn. This is in Pevsner's words ' more like a barn than a church', and the gallery is very drunken, sloping in all directions. The building is sixteenth century, with Victorian repairs. The original St Peter's was burnt down by Owain Glyndwr, but five years later a new church had been created and, apart from the east wall, it is much the same today. The timber, wattle and daub has no nails and everything is pegged together.

It has a chained bible. The black and white effect inside must make concentration on the service difficult for both priest and people, rather like praying on a square sail ship, hopefully at anchor, though on a stormy night there must be a fear of church, priest and people all being pitched into the river. Call in the sons of Noah to check it floats.

The church Orders of Service on special occasions, 1739-1900, are still in existence and include: The Jacobite Rebellion, the 1756 earthquake, Queen Victoria's safe delivery in childbirth, the Crimean War and the Indian Mutiny, Queen Victoria's Jubilees and the Boer War.

Langley Chapel

This chapel stands in a field close to Acton Burnell and was the family chapel of the Lees, whose gatehouse stands nearby. It is late Elizabethan and has a wooden bellcote. The pews include one for musicians and the minister's carved pew with tester is arranged so he can see his congregation and, if they are in a draught, he is not. There is another pulpit which is movable. The strange arrangement of pews round the altar table is for the elders to sit around the altar. I asked the Vicar if it had anything to do with communion. He said it had more to do with stating to the priest who was or was not suitable to receive it at the time the chapel was built. Perhaps as it is still consecrated, English Heritage, unlikely owners of this chapel, could hold a few more services in this delightful building. The Sunday in September when I called coincided with the once a year 3pm evensong, with a splendid tea afterwards in the field. There were 27 adults, three children and a noisy wasp. The Vicar preached on responsibility and said, 'Where your treasure is, there will your heart be'. It was a memorable occasion. After the service there was a picnic tea to which the wasp brought all his sisters, cousins, and aunts! (See the back cover for a photograph of the unusual and colourful floor tiles.)

St Mary, Cold Weston

A few miles south-west of Clee St Margaret, Cold Weston Church is across a field. It has nave, chancel and bellcote with a plain Norman north doorway, Norman chancel south window and a tie-beam dividing the nave from the chancel.

Since the original publication of this book, this church has become a private house. It can still be seen outside from the lane.

All Saints, Shelve

A rubble stone church built in 1838 on a hill below the Stiperstones in old lead-mine country. The nave and chancel are in one and there is a narrow west tower. There is a fine east window by Joseph Bell (1897) of the Supper at Emmaus over three lights and traces on the nave floor of a former medieval church on the same site.

SOMERSET

A county I have lived in for 13 years, but it still has surprises. The smallest church is on Exmoor but it has two rivals, one near Langport and one near Yeovil so I have put in all three.

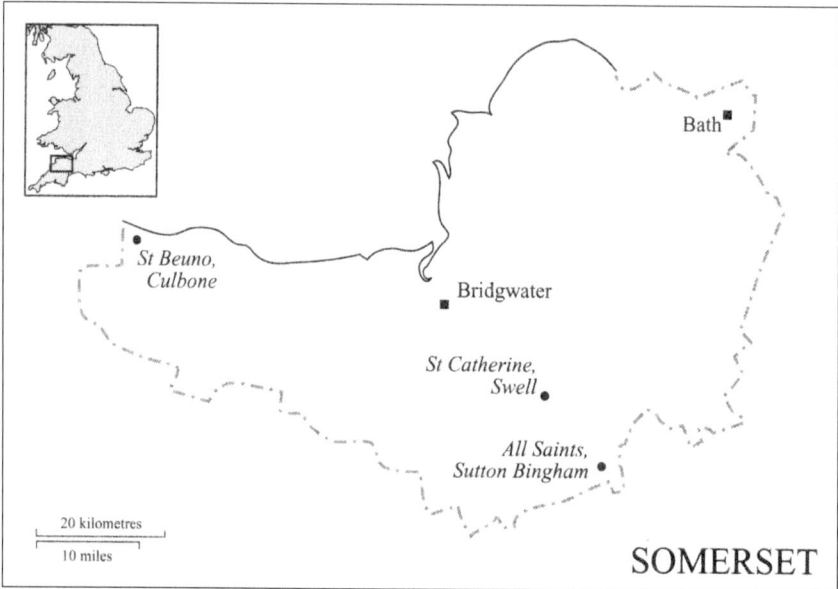

St Beuno, Culborne (near Oare)

Hidden under overhanging trees and not accessible to the motorist, Culborne Church is a delight.

Culborne is dedicated to the Welsh Saint Beuno and is part of the living of Oare and Stoke Pero. St Beuno was a Welsh saint whose cattle prospered well and his tomb at Glynnog Fawr is supposed to have remarkable healing qualities for sick children, so too his holy well.

My father-in-law was Vicar here during the last war and used to ride from Oare up the slope to cross over the Porlock–Lynmouth road to Ashley Combe Lodge where there is a path winding down to the church. His horse was tied to the cross outside the church door and one of the small congregation would make a detour if it seemed unfriendly or give it a lump of sugar, before entering the narrow nave. Here there is the Lord's Prayer and 10 commandments written up opposite the

St Beuno, Culbone. The cross has since been restored

altar. The screen is by Voysey (1928) and the east window has been over-restored much to the dislike of Pevsner.

In the sixteenth century there was a leper colony in the woods and lepers were taken there by boat. In the north wall there is a small window so lepers could look in from outside. A strange face, part cat, part man, appears on the mullion of the south window carved from one block of sandstone. With box pews, candle-lighting and a Saxon font, Culborne can surely claim to be one of the most atmospheric if not the smallest church in England. The nave length is 21ft 6in and the approximate area is 400 sq ft. There are seats for 33.

The best way to get there is to leave your car in Porlock Weir (off the A39 Bridgwater–Lynton) and take the coast path up to Culbone. The path is sometimes diverted due to coastal erosion, but is well marked. It is 2 miles uphill and obviously quicker going back. The other route from Ashley Lodge is a bit quicker, but there is not much space to leave a car in the lodge area. A nice way to travel is by steam train from Bishops Lydeard to Minehead, then bus to Porlock Weir, but the timetables need to be closely examined first. Beware of the train driver, because if it is a friend of mine who is learning, he is liable to stop before you reach the station and it is a long walk on the track.

St Catherine, Swell

Tucked away down a small lane near Langport, St Catherine is next door to the Manor House and farm. It is mostly fourteenth century and yet was a Norman church originally. The nave is about 40ft long and the walls bend alarmingly. In the 1920s, metal struts were put in the roof; further repairs were carried out in 1958, when the old box pews were removed.

On the floor is a brass which states 'Here lyeth the body of John Tooze Esq who was married to Agnes the daughter of Thomas Newton Esq, having issue by her XIV sonnes and VI daughters. He deceased the X day of June 1563.' This might account for the fact that our neighbour was a Mr J. Toze when we lived nearby and that the New Zealand cricketer Roger Toze was at school in Taunton and his family live in the area. It is a big family.

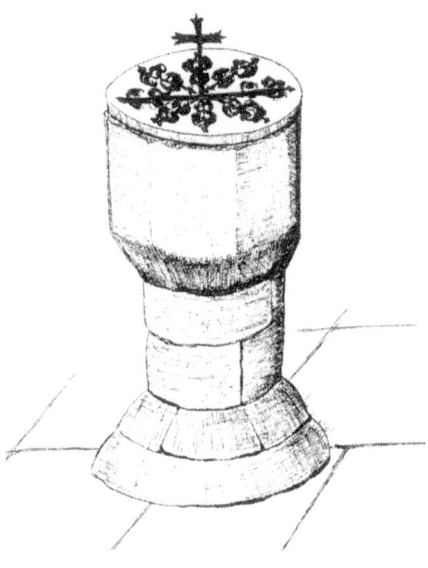

Swell Church font. *Courtesy of Alison Poole*

The church registers, it seems, are in Latin, in beautiful copperplate script, and refer to deceased persons being buried in wool during Charles II's reign to

St Catherine, Swell. *Courtesy of Alison Poole*

encourage the woollen manufacturing industry. In the East window there are small faces with tongues sticking out, perhaps because the glazier was surrounded by local children when he worked.

This is a peaceful spot. The church warden is an American navy man and at Christmas there is a candlelit service when all 40 seats are full and the little church springs into life. Long may it continue to do so.

All Saints, Sutton Bingham

This is a tiny church, similar in many ways to Swell, and it is on the other side of the main road (Yeovil–Dorchester) to Dorset's smallest church, Stockwood St Edwold, which can be seen at the same time (see p.40). To find Sutton Bingham, take the road from Yeovil (A37) and follow the sign to East Coker. At the end of the village turn right and you come to a large reservoir (this was Sutton Bingham village). As soon as you reach the other side, turn left through the trees and the church is on your right, well hidden. It is late Norman, with a fine chancel arch, three orders of columns and some fourteenth-century wall paintings. These represent the Death of the Virgin and in the chancel the Coronation of the Virgin with other bishops and saints in the windows and elsewhere.

Our sole occupant was an impatient swallow that couldn't find the way out. The grass had been cut and all was ready for a Sunday service so maybe the swallow wouldn't have too long to wait as it was Saturday evening.

All Saints, Sutton Bingham. *Courtesy of Alison Poole*

STAFFORDSHIRE

Famous for its potteries, but in fact there are some pleasant rural parts of this somewhat tourist-neglected county.

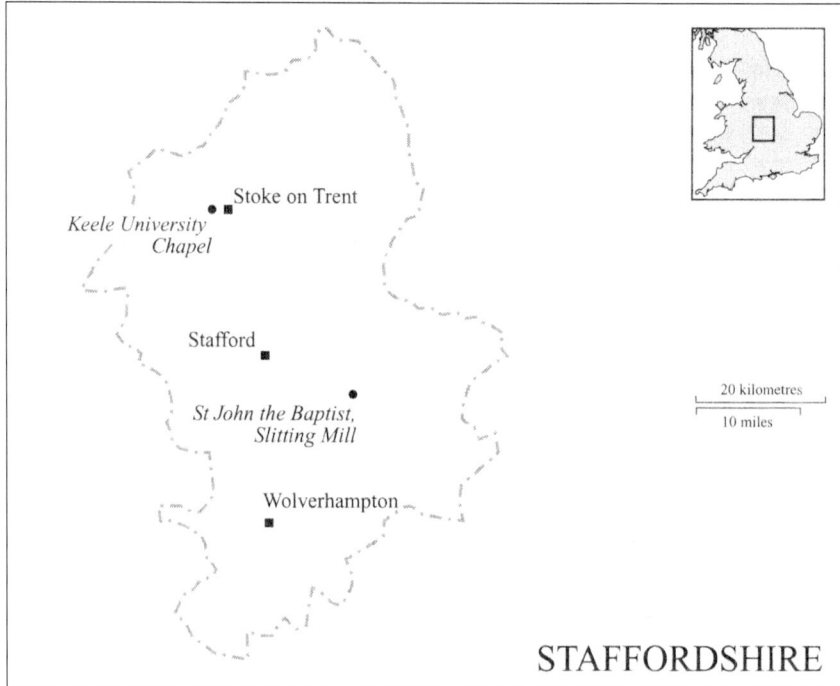

St John the Baptist, Slitting Mill

The diocese of Lichfield suggested their smallest church was at Slitting Mill. This was useful information but it needed at least two extra items. Firstly, where was Slitting Mill? And secondly, what was a 'slitting mill'? The office said 'near Rugeley' and the man in the garage said 'Posh side of town' when I asked for directions. It is a small hamlet 1¼ miles south-west and the church is down a dead-end lane attached, literally, to a yellow cottage.

It started in 1892 as an attachment to the School House. The founder was a Miss Hopkins, sister to the ironmaster of the slitting mill, where the cloth was slit into two, and the place was called Stonehouse then. The yellow cottage was for the schoolmistress and Miss Hopkins left money for her wages – £15 a year out of the sum of £600, which was not inconsiderable in 1844. The school was enlarged when the church opened with a second storey behind the Bell Tower. This room was described in a recent quinquennial report as 'A void to which there is no access' which takes some beating. In 1896, there was a new school and the church building became a Sunday school. In 1902, a sum of £18 14s 2d was spent on the triple stained-glass window which depicts the Virgin Mary (right), Crucifixion (centre) and St John the Baptist (left). In 1905 there was a definite separation of church and school and in 1972 a Mr Wheildon gave the church a new bell which came from Hagley Hall stables. One wonders if passing horses flocked to the church regardless of the wishes of their riders.

Outside the church is attached to the cottage next door, so it doesn't look like a church, more like a village schoolroom. The school/church in Danby, Isle of Man is the opposite and looks as if it is all a church.

The building inside is 29ft 6in long, seats about 24 on railway-style benches and is very welcoming. I was given a cup of tea and invited to the 9am service. The organist, it seems, was usually the last to arrive and has the longest journey so often the first hymn is well under way before the organ gets going. A small church it may be, but Slitting Mill is by far the friendliest church I have seen in my journeys whilst writing this book. Long may it continue.

Keele University Chapel

This is an ugly building, very modern in style, designed by G.G. Pace in 1964. There is no reason to include it in a book on small churches, except for one thing. The twin towers each contain chapels which are now merged into one and used daily during term time. The original idea of Mr Pace was to have one for Free Church worshippers and one for Roman Catholics, but the partition between the two has been knocked down and the Roman Catholic altar is now used for the 'Early Bird' service which is ecumenical. There is a screen that operates on the press of a button to connect the chapel with the Anglican main chapel and another screen in front of the altar. There are seats for about 45 students in a circle and three chaplains. It seems to work well. Thus the architect intended to create a small space for Roman Catholics, a small space for Free Church (?Methodists) and a large space for Anglicans. In reality they all seem to come together happily for at least one service a day.

SUFFOLK

Softer than Norfolk, with some colourful houses and thatch, the churches are more varied and harder to find. But with some help from the Round Tower Society, I have found five small churches, all very different.

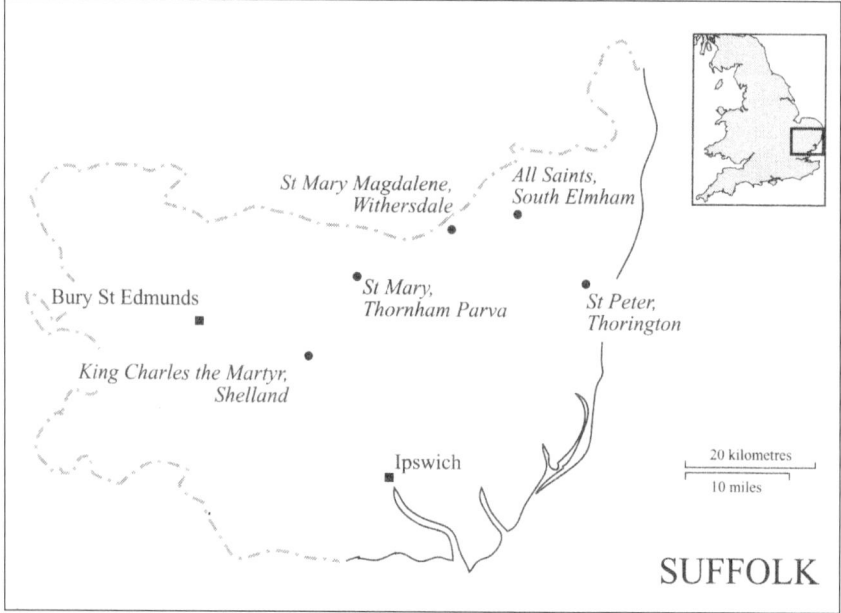

King Charles the Martyr, Shelland

Shelland is situated on a delightful green between Bury St Edmunds and Stowmarket, and has a bell turret with an ogee cap. King Charles the Martyr, Shelland is small by Suffolk standards, although the eighteenth-century pews will seat up to 60 people. The box sides are deep enough to hide behind anonymously when praying. The seats therein must be very uncomfortable during a long sermon. The church is a 'donative', privately owned, and the owner in 1646, a Royalist, Thomas Cropley, dedicated it to King Charles the Martyr, one of four churches so dedicated in England. The Ray family took over from the Cropleys and their shield can be seen over the east window.

Dr Bussell of Braesnose College, Oxford, purchased it in 1896 and gave the job of re-decoration to the local wainwright. Wagons were brightly painted in those

King Charles the Martyr, Shelland

days and the church must have looked strange. The blue ceiling may date from this period. In 1971, paler shades of paint were used, as the Vicar says 'making it more pleasing and restful to the eye.'

There is a two-decker pulpit with reading desk and clerk's pew making it a bit of an obstacle course to get there. On the south wall are wig pegs, not for visiting judges, but for eighteenth-century gentry in hot weather. One hopes they went home in the right wig! The church bell dates from 1624 and was made by Mr Cheese of Bury. The font is fourteenth century and is engraved with the shields of the Debden family which also appear in the nave windows.

The most unusual item in Shelland Church, however, is the barrel organ. It dates from 1810 and was made by Bryceson of London. It stands 7ft high and has three barrels, each of which plays 12 tunes. As you turn the handle, the six stops and 31 notes govern both volume and tune. No monkey present, but visitors come from far and wide to see and hear it played.

The smallest Suffolk church is:

St Mary, Thornham Parva

A few miles from Eye off the main A140 Norwich–Ipswich road, Thornham is a tiny hamlet with a thatched tower and nave, described by a friend as a 'Mrs Tiggy-Winkle church' that could have been used by Beatrix Potter as a source of inspiration.

The way in is not via the porch, but via the small north nave door which opens in a rush. Inside, the most famous item is the fourteenth-century retable (a painted panel set in a reredos) which was discovered in the stable of Thornham Hall in 1927 and dated mid-fourteenth century. It shows Saints Dominic, Catherine, John, Peter, Paul, Edmund, Margaret of Antioch and Peter the Martyr. In the middle, between Peter and Paul, is the Crucifixion. The nave measures 36ft 7in, there are wall paintings showing St Edmund and the wolf. These are on the north wall and have been restored, but not repainted. They are:

1. St Edmund attempts to flee the Danes
2. His Martyrdom
3. His head is re-joined to his body
4. The burial procession accompanied by the wolf
5. The cart crosses a bridge (this one is clearly visible)

The Whistler window is in memory of Lady Olga Henniker-Major (1974) and quotes Psalm 33: 'Full many a glorious morning have I seen flatter the mountain tops with sovereign eye.'

Outside in the churchyard is the grave of Sir Basil and Lady Spence, architect of the new Coventry Cathedral. As a final touch, instead of buying a guidebook, you can spend a pound on a pound of home-made marmalade which is an original method of fundraising for the upkeep of this little gem of a church.

St Mary, Thornham Parva

In the spring of 2003 the remarkable retable came home to the church after a £130,000 restoration. The timber was analysed and it was found it came from Poland and the red pigment from an insect found on the Polish coast – the first time this colour has been identified on a British painting.

All Saints, South Elmham

This is a middle-Saxon church with a round tower, and it is quite hard to find as there are no less than seven South Elmhams. All Saints is in St Nicholas parish and is a redundant church, approached by a farm road then a footpath beside a field. There is space for one car to park and then a notice had been posted, presumably by the farmer, rearranging the approach to the church. Two recent burials might have made this of importance. The nave is 26ft 3in, but there is an aisle, so although All Saints may be the smallest round tower church in Suffolk, it is quite large inside. There was much restoration in 1870 and yet the Saxon ledge to the thin west wall is still there, the tower has six windows without dressed stone and there is one bell dated 1603. What made my visit in early July really delightful was seeing the mass of wild flowers growing in the churchyard, including orchids, which the grass cutter had been careful to preserve.

Other small churches to see in Suffolk:

St Peter, Thorington

This is a round tower church with a 32ft nave. It is not far from Blythburgh. The tower has strange sixteenth-century brick battlements and an unfortunate showy neo-Norman arch. There is an octagonal marble font with four seated lions on the stem. Some of the benches have poppy heads.

St Mary Magdalene, Withersdale

Not far from Harleston, Withersdale Church has a near perfect seventeenth-century interior of two-decker pulpit, box pews and Jacobean communion rails. Outside it has a weatherboarded bell-turret, nave and chancel. There are two Norman windows and a Norman doorway.

SURREY

Surrey is a county I know well, having been brought up there and spent much time walking on Blackdown, driving down leafy lanes, attending a rather dull Victorian church and commuting up to London. However, the three churches chosen, or two chapels and a church, were all new to me and a real surprise. Taking the A3 as a link, the first church is a high street one.

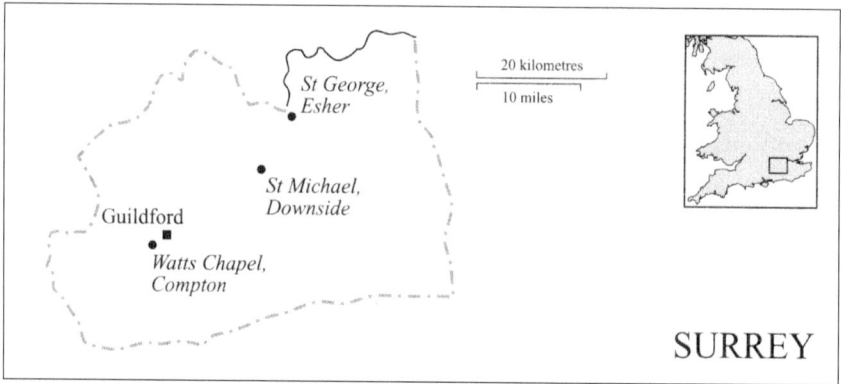

St George, Esher

No longer used more than six times a year (for choral evensong) St George's is the 1540 ex-parish church used by the village of Esher until the building of the 1854 Victorian church on the other side of the road. You have to call here first to obtain the two keys to get in. The church is made of stone and brick, and has diagonal buttresses at the corners. Lutyens would have approved of the wooden pyramid-topped bell tower and vestry chimneys. The vestry covers the old entrance and, inside, the box pews were removed in 1908.

The most interesting item in the church is the Newcastle pew. This was built in 1725 by Vanburgh for the Duke of Newcastle and his brother Henry Pelham. It was entered directly from the outside so they didn't have to mix with the congregation (and could sleep below the parapet in the sermon, presumably). However, at the same time a three-decker pulpit was built so the preacher was high up and could see young Pelham asleep. Later, the two big local houses, Claremont and Esher Place, divided the pew. In 1816, Prince Leopold, Queen Victoria's favourite uncle, and his young wife, Princess Charlotte, came to Claremont and used the church. She died in childbirth and he went on to become King of the Belgians. Their monument by

Williamson is on the west wall and it shows the couple dispensing charity to the poor of Esher (centre), Charlotte on her deathbed (left) and Leopold accepting the Crown of Belgium (right). The figure of Britannia (the Queen?) looks on with approval.

St George's has two galleries. The bottom one was used by children and the top one gives access to the bells. The nave is about 55ft long and so St George's is not very small. It is looked after by the Churches Conservation Trust.

St Michael's Chapel, Downside, Cobham

The Guildford Diocese told me their smallest church is St Michael's, Downside. This is an estate hamlet built round a large common just over the river from Cobham. The Coombe estate in 1858 built a pump for drinking water and a bakehouse next to it. Strangely, there is no sign of a chimney so perhaps there was some sort of open-air cooker. Today, the bakehouse garden is the chapel garden, for in 1955 when nearby St Matthew, Hatchford went into disuse (Pevsner calls it 'bad') and was dismantled as unsafe, the Revd Charles Wall took over the bakehouse which seats 33 (more squeezed in at Christmas) and only measures 20ft x 15ft. There is no space for kneelers, only a tiny piano and no windows open so on hot days the door has to be propped open. The altar is across the top left-hand corner (north-east) and communicants have to stand. The church is a surprise as from the outside it looks just like a bakehouse or something put up by the water board.

The lady church warden told us that there are plans to build an apse, vestry and a 'washroom', so presumably the altar will have to be placed in the apse. One hopes that a sympathetic architect is chosen, as this delightful and very moving chapel, part of the United Benefice of East Horsley, Ockham, Hatchford and Downside, has an atmosphere that needs to be kept intact. The Vicar, Revd Paradise, will hopefully see to this: 'I could not possibly worship in a large church' was the comment of the church warden.

To see this chapel you have to apply to the Church Office at Ockham for a key, or attend a Sunday service.

Watts Chapel, Compton

G.F. Watts, the painter and sculptor, was born in 1817 and studied in the Royal Academy. His style was influenced by Titian and he specialized in grand allegorical themes. His most famous picture *Hope* (1886) is in the Tate Gallery and is rather ambiguous in meaning. He died in 1904, hence the memorial chapel and the nearby shop and museum (closed Mondays).

It is easily found from the A3 and open all the year. Outside, the red brick chapel on its hill looks rather like an electricity sub-station. It is in the shape of a Greek cross with four curved walls. Ian Nairn (in Pevsner) says Watts did not use Art Nouveau in his paintings, but inside the effect is quite astonishing. Watts may not have approved, but the visitor is given an unusual delight. Mrs Watts had a gesso-decorated chapel built which has a diameter of 23ft. It is made of red, greens, blues and in the centre is a reproduction of *The All Rewarding* by Watts.

Charles Rennie Mackintosh would feel at home here though it lacks his clarity. Unfortunately, we visited this chapel on a Thursday, when the chapel gallery is closed, so there was no-one to sell us a guidebook. On leaving, a large fox loped across the hill as if to say that this was a rural area and he was safe now to live here with hunting seeming to be as much of the past as the painting of G.F. Watts.

The village church, St Nicholas, Compton, is unique in having a two-storeyed sanctuary and for those of you who don't like Watts, there is much to see here although it is not a small church.

SUSSEX (EAST)

Sussex has been divided into two, but still retains its distinctive character, with flint stone common in churches in both halves of the county.

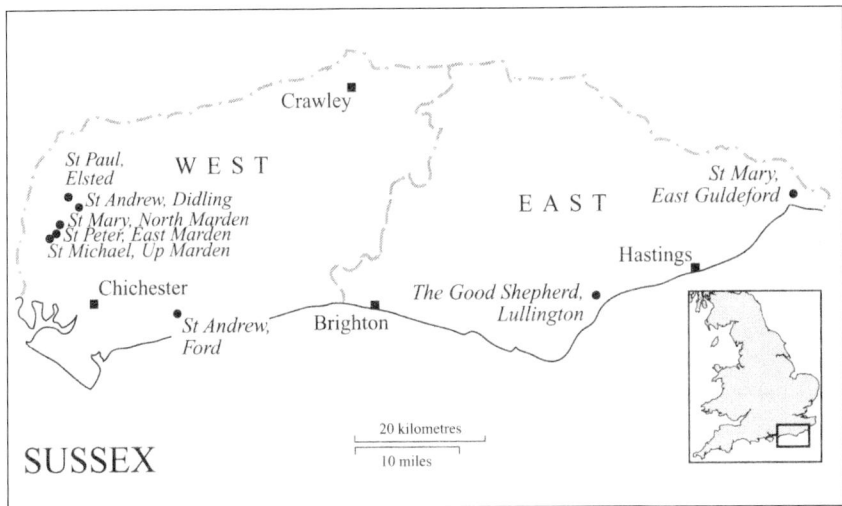

The Good Shepherd, Lullington

Near Alfriston, and without any doubt the smallest church in Sussex with 22 seats and only 16ft square, Lullington is only a chancel, like Leigh in Wiltshire. It is quite difficult to find, as someone had knocked down the sign to it when I visited. Follow the road from Alfriston towards Lullington and head up towards the Downs. There is an opening beside two garages where a small brick-lined footpath snakes into the trees and up to the church. There is a very recent (2000) dedication to The Good Shepherd but, according to a sixteenth-century will, Mr Jeg Hunt states: 'I leave a taper sett before Saint Sitha in the same church.' Saint Sithe is reckoned to be St Sitha or Zita, patron saint of housewives, being adept at baking, finding lost keys, or helping those in danger crossing rivers.

There are five windows, four of the fourteenth century, and some stones left of the old nave. It is believed the church was damaged during the Civil War by Cromwell's troops, with the nave being completely destroyed. In 1935 a replica was erected in the USA as a war memorial, but no-one seems to know where. The west end of the church is modern, but well-constructed in flint with two sloping buttresses. There didn't seem to be a light, but the double doors give plenty of light and the churchyard was immaculate.

Lullington has a sacred atmosphere and with its white weather-boarded belfry and cross it is an unusual sight. Why was it never restored? There were vicars from 1356 to 1927, the Registers date from 1721. It was repaired in 1806 and again in 1894 and has services at 3pm on the third Sunday of every month. At Harvest Festival, half the congregation have to be accommodated outside the church. There is barely room for 20 inside and, although only half a church, it must qualify as the smallest used half in the country.

Another church to see in East Sussex:

St Mary, East Guldeford

This is one of the Romney Marsh churches that escaped over the border into Sussex. It is a plain square building with a low roof made of brick in 1505. It has a long nave, brick floor and box pews. There is a George IV Royal Arms as well as metal beams to support the roof because the whole building stands on a marsh. Sir Richard Guldeford was a supporter of Henry Richmond, later King Henry VII. His coat of arms on the north wall has three rosettes to remind us of this. Behind the altar is a mural of angels holding pictures of the six days of Creation outlined in Genesis.

SUSSEX (WEST)

There are some interesting downland churches near the border with Hampshire, all unique and well worth visiting. Firstly there are the Marden churches near the Hampshire border on the way to South Harting if you are coming from Rye. Like Nately Scures, the smallest is North Marden, St Mary, hidden away and sited beside a farm.

St Mary, North Marden

St Mary is a single-cell apsidal like Winterbourne Tomson, but is in regular use. The church is well surrounded by trees, as if the farmer wanted to disown it. There is a long footpath down to it beside the farm drive, but it is small enough to be invisible until you are almost on top of it. Inside it has a plain Norman font like a large egg-cup with a lead interior and, round the south doorway, a zigzag moulding. A Norman church with a trefoiled piscine and an iron Royal Arms of George III, St Mary is the baby of the Mardens.

St Mary, North Marden. *Courtesy of A.J. Robinson*

St Peter, East Marden

More attractive is St Peter, East Marden, which has an unusual early nineteenth-century organ from Tottenham Court Road, London. It has a sliding finger board and I was given a private recital which was quite moving. On the north wall is a tapestry showing the Marden farms, houses and two churches. Fred Griggs, author of *Highways and Byways in Sussex*, visited East Marden in 1903. He said it had 'the most modest and least ecclesiastical-looking church in the world' and that the village was the finest place for white violets and for keeping a horse. Alas, it had no pub. He walked to Stoughton, which had a good inn, and where George Brown, the fast bowler, lived. Born in Stoughton, Brown 'had two long stops, one of whom padded his chest with straw... the ball once went through his coat (the straw man's) and killed a dog on the other side'. Brown could throw a 4½oz ball 137 yards and was the father of 17 children. He died in 1857. England could do with more bowlers like him, especially on tours to Australia.

St Michael, Up Marden

Missing is the gem of all Marden churches (in a different parish) which is St Michael's, Up Marden. Ian Nairn describes it as 'the atmosphere is as tangible as any moulding, the slow, loving, gentle accretion century by century until it is something as organic as any of the South Downs views around it ... it is incredibly moving whether one is Anglican or not, whether one is religious or not.' The effect of clear glass, wagon-wheel style candelabra, brick floors, white walls and an unspoilt thirteenth-century interior makes this a church worth going miles to see. It is not really a qualifier for the smallest church, but it is certainly the most atmospheric.

St Andrew, Didling

Take the A286 south from Haslemere and Midhurst, then turn right at Cocking. The little church of St Andrew is up a lane leading to the South Downs. Outside, the church has a roof covering both nave and chancel and there is a clear area round the flint-stone walls for preventing damp. The doorway has a bird screen, but one feels birds might be quite welcome in this church, known as 'The Shepherd's church' because of its position.

We called just before Harvest Festival, so everything was beautifully decorated inside. The heavy benches sprouting candles, tub font and Jacobean communion rail all breathed an atmosphere of care and trust. The nave and chancel are together, the lighting is by oil lamps or candles and restorers have been careful to respect the original creators of this charming little church. Outside, the massive yew tree was once threatened with being cut down, but a passer-by stopped this from happening. So many important aspects of Christianity are due to passers-by. The one at Didling is no exception.

Other churches to see in West Sussex:

St Paul, Elsted

Not far from Harting, Elsted Church has gone through some serious problems. In Victorian times, a new church was built at Treyford and Elsted fell into disuse. Worse than that, a tree fell on the nave in 1893. It was restored in 1951 after a lot of fundraising. Note the herringbone walling of the eleventh-century, especially on the north wall. The chancel is like Didling, very simple and dating to the thirteenth century, and the new nave has a lean-to vestry and a rather unsympathetic hexagonal west window.

St Andrew, Ford

Not far from Littlehampton, Ford is a simple nave and chancel church close to Ford Open Prison, once a Fleet Air Arm base. The building is basically Norman, but the porch is 1637 with a Dutch gable. John Vigar has pointed out that there are two painted consecration crosses in the nave which may be of pre-Conquest date and there are other crosses on the south door done by medieval graffiti artists, as well as mass dials outside.

WARWICKSHIRE

Shakespeare's county is surprisingly tree-covered, *Arden* is the name for a forest and most buildings are well looked-after, villages neat and tidy and there is a lot for all visitors to see. However, the smallest church is sadly neglected, closed and yet is historically interesting. This is at Billesley.

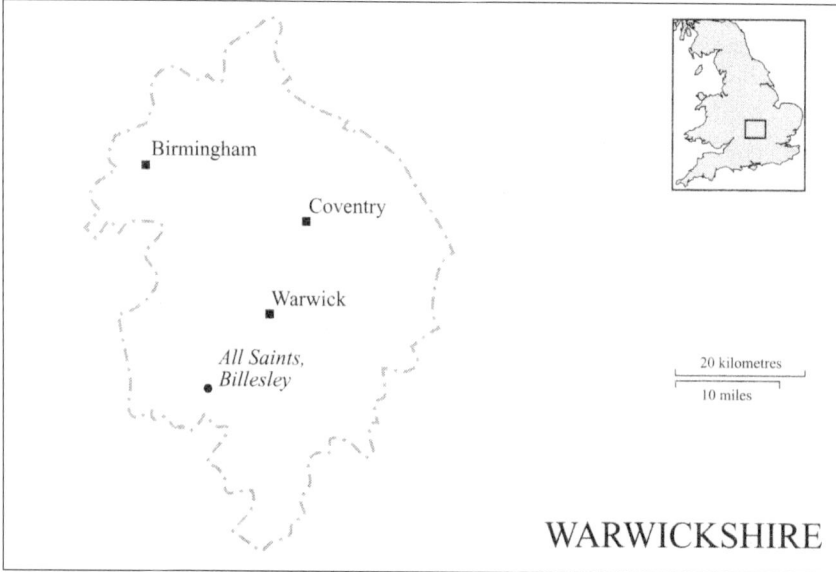

All Saints, Billesley

Just off the A422 Stratford–Alcester road, Billesley Trussel is the site of a deserted medieval village. Shakespeare would have known it and rumour has it that this is where he married Anne Hathaway. However, the medieval village and old church vanished with the Black Death, and a new church was constructed in 1692 out of the remaining stones. It has an apse, a 30ft nave and box pews including one, lined in red cloth, with a fireplace. There is a vestry, presumably the original entrance from the manor house, now a hotel. We went there for the key, which has a brass fob picture, inappropriately of Queen Mary, and there is a wooden gate from the manor car park to the church lane.

In the nineteenth century one Revd Knottesford came from his home at Alveston by carriage, with his picnic lunch and children if fine, for the 11 o'clock matins. The curate took the service, the rector preached and the children then played outside while the rector ate his lunch in front of the fire. Then at 3pm there was evensong and the family all went home.

Today, the lime trees have been trimmed to poles, the nettles are head high and the church is vested in the Churches Conservation Trust. Note the Mills family monuments — they lived next door — the unusual tympanum in the vestry and Harrowing Stone, which experts liken to the Herefordshire (Kilpeck) school of sculpture.

There is another little church well worth a visit. The Diocesan Office recommended St Michael, Baddesley Clinton, situated in a field about 250 yards from the moated manor house. It is too large for our purposes, a Ferrers Church, and is kept locked when the Hall is shut. Inside the Hall, however, is the Sacristy, a hidden part of the chapel with a cross placed over the garderobe exit. Here in Elizabethan times the priests — for the family were then Catholics — hid, held services and, if necessary, scrambled down the wet garderobe into the moat and swam for safety.

WESTMORLAND

This county is now part of Cumbria, but Pevsner still couples it with Cumberland, and it has its own characteristics.

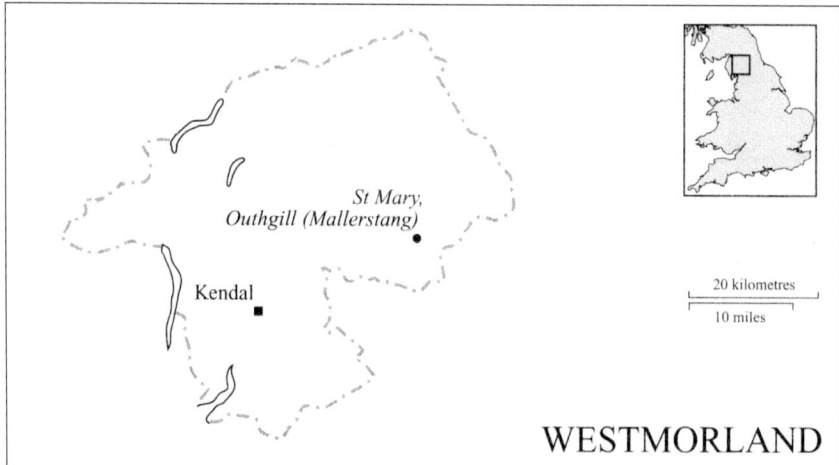

St Mary, Outhgill (Mallerstang)

To find Outhgill (Mallerstang is the name of the valley), take the road to Sedbergh, then follow the A684 to Garsdale Head, where you take the left fork for Kirkby Stephen. The road follows the railway – many of those who built it, the Settle–Carlisle line, are buried here – and eventually the church appears on the left-hand side. Walk through the churchyard, cross the stream and the key of the church can be obtained from Froth Cottage.

The history of the rebuilding in 1665 of the ruinous 'chapple' by Lady Anne Clifford is on a plaque over the doorway. The cost was £46 15s 6d. She purchased land near Sedbergh to endow the church and only recently has it been sold. Inside there is a Charles II coat of arms, a font resembling a sharp pencil top, seating for about 60 persons and a nave length of 30ft 4in. There is a large 1926 window showing a labourer pruning a vine to commemorate John Thornborrow who was church warden for 40 years. He must have been very clever to keep vines in this part of the world. There are two 10.30am services a month, on the second and fourth Sundays, and it was nice to see on the wall a photograph of the previous curate whom I had known in the gentler climate of Somerset.

WILTSHIRE

Wiltshire is good county for small churches, but I have included only seven, one of which is very small indeed.

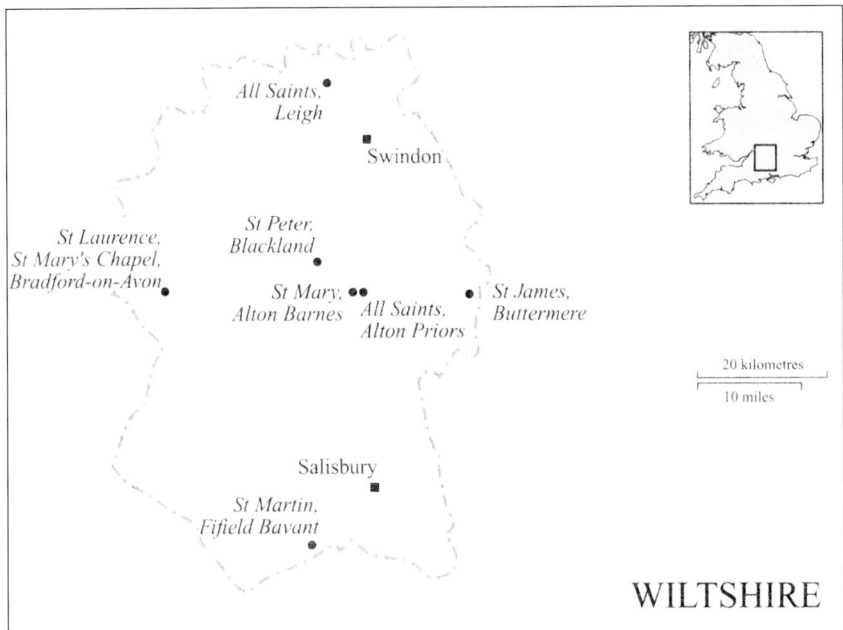

St Martin, Fifield Bavant

The smallest parish church in Wiltshire, St Martin, Fifield, stands in a field at the back of stables. Outside this church has a stock-proof fence to keep out the horses and it has a fairly recent tile-hung bell-turret topped with a cockerel weather-vane. The door has gone from the north side and there is a cross over the east gable.

The nave and chancel are all one. Inside there is a Norman font, one thirteenth-century lancet window and on the other side a three-light seventeenth-century one. The cane chair by the altar has recently been restored by a Mr Arnold, who was presented it by two elderly sisters who told him that it came from the church back in the 1920s. It looks very much more comfortable than the pews. There is a tile-hung bell tower and when I visited the church, though isolated, it seemed well cared for. At nearby Alvediston is the grave of Sir Anthony Eden.

Buttermere: St James' Church from the north-west in 1806

St James, Buttermere

Much harder to find, and according to Pevsner a competitor for Wiltshire's smallest church, Buttermere lies about 4 miles from Ham on the Wiltshire/Berkshire/Hampshire border. It is in a wooded dip well off the road.

The nave and chancel again are one, but the former measures 30ft x 18ft (Fifield is only 25ft x 16ft) and there are seats for about 60. A notice states that '£50 was granted towards rebuilding of the church (in 1855 by R.J. Withers) on the condition that 15 seats numbered should be reserved for poorer inhabitants'. Someone had placed the Kipling poem on the notice board, four lines of which read:

> But three are gathered together
> List to me and attend
> I bring good news my brethren
> Said Eddi of Mahood End

The spiret has recently been restored, but the bell hangs at the back of the church wall and there is still much work to be done. The visitors' book has names from New Zealand and other far-off places, so maybe the Revd Leigh-Hunt will get his restoration money. He has an even smaller church amongst his collection – the red brick one at Bagshot – but alas it was firmly locked and there was no-one around to let us inside.

St Laurence, Bradford-on-Avon

This little church, unused and rather desolate, was only discovered by Canon Jones, a keen archaeologist, in 1856. There was a school in one part and the other had become a cottage covered in ivy. The porch had a staircase and a chimney stack

St Laurence, Bradford-on-Avon, Wiltshire © *R. W. Naesmyth of Posso*

replaced the chancel arch. The canon was doing some research in the Bodleian Library, Oxford, in 1871, when he came across a book in Latin by William of Malmesbury dated 1121. In it was a passage that said 'to this day at that place there exists a little church which Aldhelm is said to have built to the name of the most blessed Laurence.' Reading further, he noted 'a third Monastery was erected by Aldhelm at Bradford.' This was enough for him to connect it with what he had discovered fifteen years earlier.

The porch for many years was full of stones found buried nearby. Those that seemed to be Saxon were used to build the altar in 1970, but some authorities think they were part of the shrine to St Edward the Martyr, half-brother to King Ethelred. Other stones may be from the funeral procession of St Aldhelm for his body was carried from Doulting to Malmesbury with seven crosses erected at each stop and one of these was Bradford.

A Lebanese expert in 1957 visited the church and found signs of early and late Saxon tool marks in the stone working. The measurements of the building area:

Nave: 25ft 2in x 13ft 2in
Chancel: 13ft 2in x 10ft
Porch: 9ft 11in x 10ft 5in

In height, the nave is 25ft 3in, the chancel 18ft and the porch 15ft. Simon Jenkins says that the chapel would be improved with some furniture and I go further to say it should be used for an occasional service.

Up the hill there is a T-shaped hospice and chapel known as St Mary, High Tory. This is a small chapel on the hill overlooking the town. It was attached to a hermitage and in the eighteenth century it became part of a cloth factory. It was purchased and restored by Mr T.B. Saunders in 1871, when it was used as a chapel again. The easiest approach is to drive up there and walk down. It is usually open and the building looks smaller outside than in. The locals know it as the Hermit's Chapel. It has a stone tile floor, some late medieval decoration on the walls, a Victorian ceiling and two bells. Probably dating originally from the thirteenth century, St Mary's is used regularly and from outside one gets a splendid view of the town.

St Peter, Blackland

Hidden in the trees on the approach road to Calne, St Peter is close to the late Georgian mansion, Blackland Park, where the key can be obtained. The church has an aisle, much Victorian restoration dating from 1858 and some nice glass. The east window dates from 1906 and is by Kempe, showing Christ on the cross outside Jerusalem. There is much Decorated work in the windows and at one time this was in the hands of the Abbot of Malmesbury, for a note says that in 1539 the parish could provide twenty archers, five billmen, one bow and one sheaf of arrows, with the junior archer having to run out and collect arrows for his colleagues to put back in the sheaf. The billmen (or 'byllmen' as written) must have had a good laugh unless they all shared the same bill. It sounds as if Corporal Jones would have felt at home.

There is a gallery with a combined hatchment and monument to Robert Smith (d.1691) and his 'valuable wife' Margaret, who died in 1725. The four worthies

St Peter, Blackland. *Courtesy of Georgina Welch*

who restored the church all have their coats of arms in windows. They are Lord Lansdowne, Mr Pynder, Marshal Hall and Revd Macdonald. The house, which used to belong to the Wingfield-Digbys, suffered a serious fire during the war due to evacuees smoking in bed.

Other small churches to see in Wiltshire:

St Mary, Alton Barnes

A small Anglo-Saxon church beside a busy farm, but over-restored and externally rendered. The chancel was rebuilt in brick with a blue ceiling in 1748 and then it was given further alterations in 1875 and 1904. There is a three-decker pulpit, a heraldic stained-glass window to W. Lamplugh, 1737, and outside it is a short walk over the fields to Alton Priors. (See page 154).

All Saints, Alton Priors

Unused and looked after by the Churches Conservation Trust since 1972. There is a perpendicular west tower, some box pews, a tomb chest and a brass to William Button, 1590, put there by his grandson.

All Saints, Leigh

Close to Ashton Keynes is a wet field with the chancel of All Saints Church. The Vicar and PCC in 1896 decided to build a new church on drier ground, so the nave was moved stone by stone. The arches and windows date from the thirteenth and fifteenth centuries, and there is a bench for the service once a year, usually in July, when the congregation is asked to bring musical instruments. The structure is cared for very well by the Churches Conservation Trust and like Lullington, West Sussex, it must qualify for the smallest half-church in the country even if rarely used.

There are 18 other churches in Wiltshire looked after by the Trust and their useful green leaflet can be obtained at Leigh or by writing with an SAE to 8 All Saints Street, London N1 9RL.

WORCESTERSHIRE

John Betjeman describes the county as a fruit tart, the centre all orchards and blossom in spring, the edges are wooded hills. The part nearest Birmingham is black for the Black Country. This is apt but it does not mention the Upper Teme Valley which is real country.

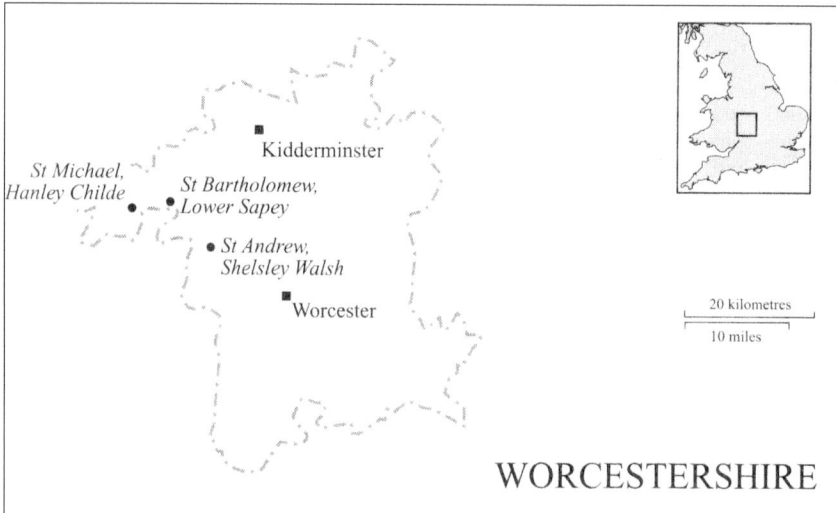

St Michael, Hanley Childe

The village, or hamlet, just two farms and a couple of cottages, is off the Worcester to Tenbury Wells road. The church is approached by a grassy track fringed by daffodils in spring time. When I called in March a man was cutting down two fruit trees in the field next door where the sheep seemed unsurprised. The view over Herefordshire and Shropshire from here is magnificent.

St Michael's is long and low, dating from 1807. The sandstone is cut by three plain glass windows with metal grills to protect them. They let in the light, but seem a bit too large for the size of the church. Nineteenth-century altar rails and pews for about 40 churchgoers survive. There used to be a tower, but it collapsed in 1864, so now there are two doors and a bellcote. The outer door has a large gap – for swallows to get in and out perhaps – and the whole rural scene is remarkably peaceful. The nave is over 40ft long but it is smaller than Hanley William about a mile away on the other side of the main road.

St Bartholomew, Lower Sapey

On the way back to Worcester, look in at St Bartholomew, Lower Sapey near Clifton-on-Teme. This is empty of all furniture, has a gallery and is looked after by the Churches Conservation Trust. Its last service was held on hay bales and when I called the door was wide open to allow the bats to get in and out.

Near here too is St Andrew, Shelsley Walsh. A village known to all motor racing and hill climbing folk, but a church that is constructed of tufa, has a tie-beam and collar beam chancel roof, and a screen and parclose screen. One wonders what happens when the sermon coincides with a noisy hill climb. Maybe the Vicar tries to avoid services clashing with such events. In Somerset once we persuaded 40 cyclists to attend Morning Service in their black shorts, water bottles and singlets, before their race. Maybe the congregation at Shelsley Walsh comes dressed in leather skull-caps and goggles.

YORKSHIRE (EAST)

The vast county of Yorkshire is conveniently divided into three. The West has the Dales and some of the churches are very remote. The North has York with some splendid villages, all well looked after, but few small churches. The East with its sea coast gets smaller every year. Some summers ago I went to a hotel in Scarborough with my mother, who had known it in the 1930s. She said the rose garden would take half an hour to see. It took five minutes. The following year the entire hotel slipped into the sea.

The East Riding, to most people, has two small churches that are worth describing in detail. One of them is hard to find and having found it once with the help of the Vicar of Rudston who looks after it as well, I doubt if I will find it again.

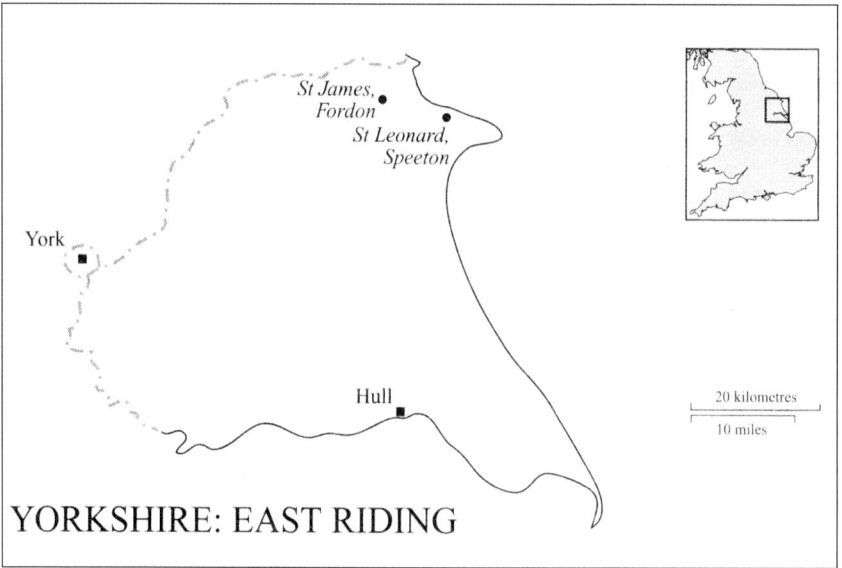

St James, Fordon

The church of St James, Fordon is at a crossroads in the Wolds north of Wold Newton. There is a farm nearby, but otherwise no other signs of habitation. St James was built as a chapel of ease to All Saints, Hunmanby. It has a Norman door with a carved pattee and windows dating from 1768 in Gothic. In 1876, a vestry was built – now in need of a new roof – and the brick bell tower. In living memory it was used as a shelter for animals and in 1923 the *Bridlington Free Press* said it 'had not a single window complete, roof full of holes and the inside presents a revolting picture of desecration.'

In 1973 the interior was replastered, redecorated, electricity installed and two oak-framed windows with leaded lights put in. The east window was also restored. The result is a living little church that measures: nave 25ft 11½in x 14ft 3in and chancel 11ft x 9½in x 11ft 10in. The vestry, disused with fireplace, is 7ft 9in x 5ft 3in. There is the occasional service here but one wonders what the future is for Fordon.

St Leonard, Speeton

Speeton is a small village on the coast a few miles north of Bridlington. The church is a simple one-room building with a tower and no churchyard, standing in farmland close to the sea. After the Norman Conquest, Speeton belonged to the Augustinian Priory at Bridlington. In 1290, Edward I granted the prior and canons free wareen over Speeton and over areas nearby. There was a chaplain in 1451. During the Reformation the stone altar, vestments and statue of St Leonard, patron saint of prisoners, were all removed.

During the Commonwealth, the Chaplain was paid £3 12s 0d a year and Richard Broderick, chaplain, came from Bampton and was a Puritan. In the eighteenth century, the font was moved into the chancel and the church often stood empty. Locals think it was used as a storeroom for local smugglers. In the nineteenth century part of the church became a school. In 1852, Charlotte Brontë described it as 'not more than thrice the length of our passage, floored with brick, walls green with mould, pews painted white but the paint almost worn off with time and decay.'

The coffins used to be carried all the way to Bridlington Priory and the pall-bearers refreshed themselves at the Nag's Head. They caused a track to be made from Speeton Church which was used by villagers and others. The church had box pews until 1914 when they were replaced by small pine pews. In 1976/7, Francis Johnson, a local architect, was given the job of a more complete restoration. Oak benches and altar rails from the Hostel of the Resurrection, Leeds, were installed and the new altar rails were dedicated to the organist, Elizabeth Coleman, who died

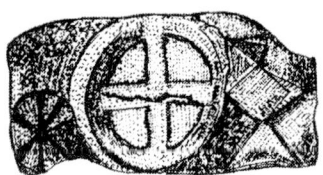

Stone bearing circular cross

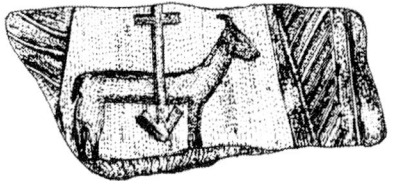

Agnus Dei

From Speeton Church guidebook

in April 1977. Shortly before this, a stone Agnus Dei and one of a circular cross were placed in the wall. They may have come from a Saxon consecration cross.

There is a stone alms box and an 11am service of Morning Prayer every Sunday. One final thought about this delightful church is, please do not park in front of it, as it spoils the view for photographers.

YORKSHIRE (NORTH)

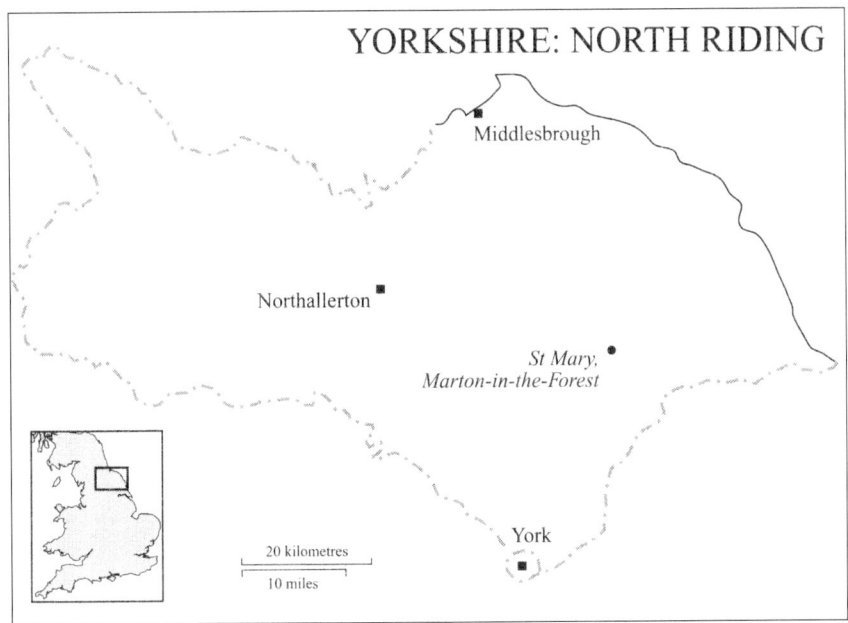

St Mary, Marton-in-the-Forest

To find this little church, take the B1363 north from York and Marton, and it is found a mile or two after Stillington. It is Marton-in-the-Forest not Marton-le-Moor or Marton near Guisborough which is Captain Cook's village. The forest near the River Foss was known as the Forest of Galtres. The church is mainly fifteenth century, with a Norman chancel arch and a tower (6ft square inside) dating from the sixteenth century. Pevsner calls it 'Perp. but violently restored.' Marton Priory nearby, when dissolved, gave up some of its stone shields and an IHC stone which are reset in the tower. The outside east and west ends have stepped gables and the stepped buttresses to the south door look like wings. Inside, the plain Jacobean pews have trefoil ends, the font is thirteenth century and the nave measures 30ft. The west window has some stained glass.

Marton comes under the Sheriff Hutton team and for Richard III addicts the church there houses the sad tomb of the seven-year-old Edward, Prince of Wales who died at Middleham and broke his mother's heart. She was Anne, queen to

King Richard III and she died a year later in 1484, her husband lasting just a few months longer before his demise at Bosworth Field.

The castle is named after its builder, Betram de Bulner, Sheriff of Yorkshire, but it was a royal castle and Richard III had put some of his prisoners here, including the attractive Elizabeth of York, daughter of his late brother's queen. He had his eye on her, but before any decision was made on her future the Battle of Bosworth intervened and the young princess became queen to Henry Richmond.

YORKSHIRE (WEST)

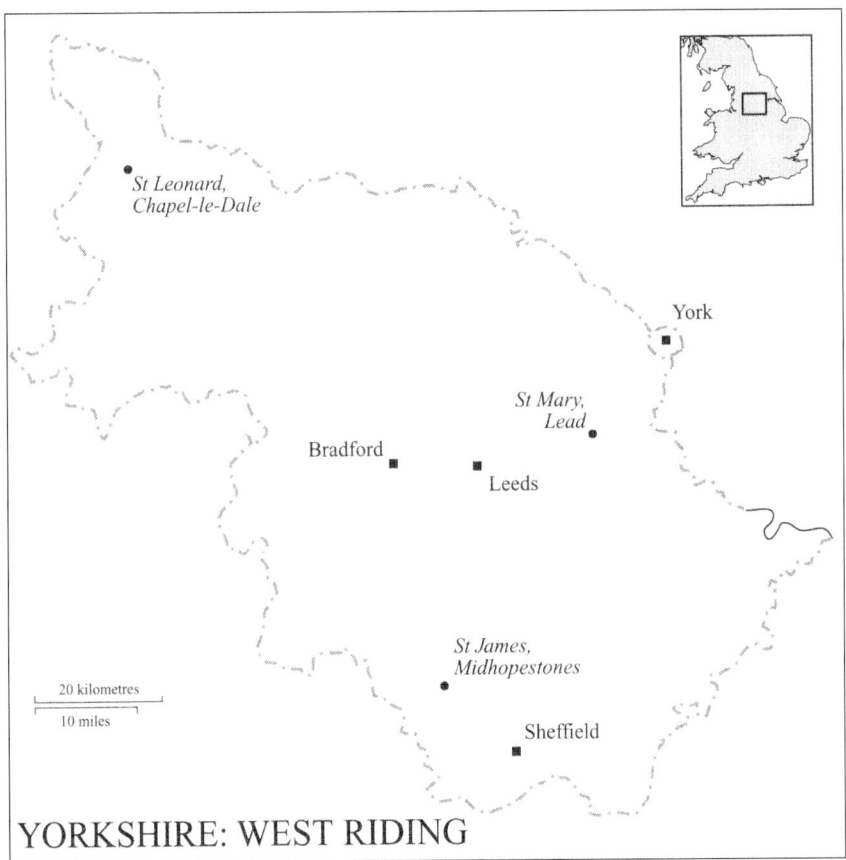

St James, Midhopestones

This church is in a village situated off the A616 between Huddersfield and Sheffield. The Mustard Pot Inn is well marked and the church is up the hill a few hundred yards from the inn. It is a lonely building with 1705 over the porch, but clearly older than this. Inside, the layout is not unlike Dale, but a bit more organised. There are box pews, two with names of owners, 'John Wilson's seat' and 'Sarah Wainwright's seat' not far away, but sufficiently far so as to imply they were not friends. There is a large gallery and an ugly font, clear glass windows (once they had green glass) and the front pews have been modernised so that the vicar had some breathing space. The pulpit, as at Dale, is to the left of the altar. The local blacksmith must have made the cross and candlesticks. Two ladies were preparing flowers for a local wedding so this is a church that, even though it only has two services a month, is not without friends.

St Mary, Lead

This is a tiny church in the middle of a field near Towton. To find it, take the road to Tadcaster and turn right in the centre of Towton, pass the battlefield cross (which when it had fallen down was repaired by an Australian builder tourist) and you come to the Crooked Billet pub. Park here and over the road is a bridge with a footpath to the church. It is now in the hands of the Churches Conservation Trust and its history is on the door. Restored in 1784 and in 1932 by some ramblers led by Jack Winterburn, it was re-dedicated in 1932 by the Bishop of Whitby (some distance away and why Whitby?) and more recently repaired by the Richard III Society who have inserted a small pane of glass in the east window. The Battle of Towton, one of the bloodiest battles of the Wars of the Roses, took place in March 1461 and Lead Chapel was a refuge for the wounded of both sides. The little river must have been a source of water and the field would have been crowded with soldiers. This explains the interest in the upkeep of the chapel by the Society. Nearby, the Tyas family had their manor and this was presumably their chapel, as their tombs are in front of the altar.

The roof bosses have been hung on the walls and the east window used to be the east window of the chancel, but the Vavasour family, who took over from the Tyas family, found it in disrepair in 1596 and removed the chancel, re-using the window, while excavators found the bosses. There are two texts, one which pleads 'Give alms of thy Good(es) and turn not thy face from anye poor man and face of ye Lord shall not be turned from thee.'

The nave is 26ft 1in long to the altar step, on which the three-decker pulpit has been constructed. It has a good claim to being Yorkshire's smallest church.

St Leonard, Chapel-le-Dale

The little church at Chapel-le-Dale is close to the Ribbleshead viaduct on the Settle–Carlisle line. It is hidden in the trees by three cottages, but is not locked and visitors are welcome. There are mullioned windows with two and three lights. The east window by Kempe is especially fine. It shows left, a lamb and flag surrounded by circles and oval shapes in the Art Nouveau style, centre is Jesus and the two Marys, and right, a swan. The blue and pink colours and black surround are most effective. Another window shows animals and shepherds looking at the baby Jesus with Mary and Joseph. Strangely, the animals are not sheep but look like young cattle or large dogs.

The nave is 31ft 8in and there is a monument to those who 'through accidents lost their lives in constructing the railways works between Settle and Dent Head' which was erected by fellow workmen and the Midland Railway Company 1849-1873.

Outside there is a Millennium monument to these workers and on our way back to the Ribblehead Viaduct a helicopter appeared with a stone attached to a long wire that it placed in the right position before flying off. The local rooks must have been surprised and so too the ghosts of the railway navvies.

GLOSSARY

Appliqué	Ornamental work where fabric is cut out and applied to the surface of other material. (*See Arne, Dorset*)
Apse	Semi-circular or polygonal recess often used as a chancel. (*See Billesley, Warkwickshire*)
Apsidal	In the curved form of an apse.
Auditory Church	One designed so congregation can hear the preacher. (*See Guyhirn, Cambridgeshire*)
Baptistery	That part of the church in which baptism takes place.
Board Bell Turret	Bell turret clad in wooden boards.
Box Pew	A pew boxed in for keeping out draughts. Some have their own fireplaces.
Broach Spire	A spire, usually octagonal, rising from a square tower. The triangular face created is the 'broach'.
Buttress	Can be angle (at each angle of the church), clasping (all round the corner), set back (near corners), diagonal (going out at angles from corners) or flying (as at St Paul's Cathedral).
Canopy Roof	A roof with a tent top (*as at Rycote, Oxfordshire*).
Chapel	Sacred buildings less than churches. A Chapel of Ease (*see Billington, Beds*) was constructed for the comfort and ease of those living some distance from their parish church. Some have since become parish churches in their own right. A Chantry Chapel was one where the founder provided money for prayers to be said for his soul and that of his family in perpetuity. Mortuary Chapels are usually located in a graveyard.
Clergy	Archbishop: Responsible for a province, i.e. York or Canterbury. Bishop: Responsible for a Diocese. They often have Suffragen Bishops to help them. There are also Flying Bishops who minister to those who are opposed to the ordination of women. Dean: One who presides over a cathedral or collegiate church. Canon: Residentiary canons have cathedral duties and non-residentiary are usually honorary canons in recognition of a diocesan service like a Director of Education. Archdeacon: Senior clergy delegated by the bishop. Rural Dean: A clergyman who supervises the running of a number of rural parishes. Deacon/Deaconess: One who has advanced to the final stage of priesthood. Rector: Once an incumbent who received tithes and was responsible for chancel, rectory and supplying service books and vestments. Lesser tithes went to a Vicar. Since the abolition of tithes (1936), a Vicar is appointed to all new livings and a Rector is appointed to team ministries, joint or united benefices. A Parson can be either a Vicar or a Rector. A Curate is an assistant priest, or an unbeneficed clergyman. Chaplains: Priests of chapels, ministering to hospitals, prisons, the armed services and as secretaries to bishops.
Collar Beam Roof	A cross beam, higher than a tie beam, across the apex of a roof.

GLOSSARY

Communion Rails	After the Reformation these were used to keep stray dogs and other animals away from the altar. (*See Fairfield, Kent*)
Consecration Cross	A cross incised in a circle, often painted red, to keep demons out of the church, usually put there when the church was consecrated. (*See Sutton Bingham, Somerset*)
Corbel	Projection of stone, brick or wood used to support a beam, screen etc. It can be decorated with a face. (*See Farndish, Bedfordshire*)
Donative	Church given to the community by a donor, sometimes without reference to the authorities.
Easter Sepulchre	A place for the sacrament to be kept, usually on the north side of the chancel, from Good Friday until Easter Sunday. There is a fine one at Tarrant Hinton, Dorset.
Family Pew	A box pew, sometimes with a fireplace and special furnishing where the squire or local nobleman sat during a service. (*See St George's, Esher*)
Hatchments	Diamond-shaped heraldic panels with the coat of arms of the deceased. They are usually placed on the wall of the church following internment. (*See Hoveton, Norfolk*)
IHC stone	A stone with the letters IHC, which are the first three letters of the word 'Jesus' in Greek, often used as a Christian symbol.
Keeil	Small stone-built rectangular chapels, mostly in ruins, in the Isle of Man. Churches are often built on their sites. (*See Ballaugh Old Church*)
Kempe Window	Windows made by Kempe – a famous Victorian stained-glass maker.
King Post	A central vertical post on a tie beam supporting the roof.
Lay Reader	Since 1866, the Church of England has licensed lay persons to conduct services that don't involve Holy Communion. They can conduct funerals but not weddings or christenings. After training they, women or men, are admitted to their office by their diocesan bishop and every year they hold a conference in Cambridge.
Lych-Gate (or Lich-Gate)	From the Old English *Lich* meaning 'corpse' and referring to the roofed gate of a churchyard. In Cornwall (*Boconnoc, Philleigh and other churches*) it is common to have a resting stone for coffins and the funeral service starts from the gate.
Maundy Money	On the Thursday of Easter Week, to commemorate the act of Christ's washing the feet of the Apostles, the sovereign distributes specially minted Maundy Money, the number of recipients corresponding to her age. There is a collection to be seen at Childwickbury, St Mary in Hertfordshire.
Minstrel Placement	Where the minstrels sat, sometimes in a special gallery.
Misericord	A hinged wooden seat which when tipped up forms a projection for the sitter to rest on when standing up. They are usually carved with heraldic beasts etc. (*See Duntisbourne Rous, Gloucestershire*)
Mullion	Vertical divide between lights (glass panels) of a window.
Ogee Cap	Cap with S-shaped curve, sometimes used at the top of a monument.
Oratory	Place of worship other than a church or chapel. It is often put to other uses today, e.g. at Bradford on Avon the bridge oratory became a lock-up. (*See The Tower of London*)
Parclose Screen	A screen between a side chapel and another part of the church.
Parish	From the Anglo-Saxon word 'parochium', the parish is the smallest unit of ecclesiastical administration.
Parvis	The room above the porch. Friar suggests this may not be correct. There is an outstanding example at St John's, Cirencester.

Pattee	Cross with ends spread like claws.
Piscina	Recess for washing holy vessels with basin and drain.
Porticus	Side chapel or porch-like chamber entered from the main body of the church.
Preaching Cross	A cross outside the church used for preaching in the open air. (See St Bega, Bassenthwaite)
Premonstratensian	White order of canons belonging to order founded in 1120 by St Norbert at Prémontré, France.
Quatrefoil	Figure with four radiating petals. They can be an edge to heraldic shields on a tomb.
Reredos	Decorative screen behind and above an altar.
Retable	A reredos (screen at the back of the altar) with painted panels, often made of material, and quite scarce today. (See Thornham Parva, Suffolk)
Rood Loft	A platform above the rood screen, often elaborately carved and used by singers or musicians. Most were removed at the Reformation. (See St Margarets, Herefordshire)
Rood Screen	Decorative screen separating chancel from nave, usually built to support a rood loft, above which was the Great Rood – a crucifixion group of the Virgin, Christ and St John the Apostle. They were removed at the Reformation.
Churches Round Tower	Common in East Anglia. For details see the excellent publications of the Round Tower Churches Society, 6 The Warren, Old Catton, Norwich, NR6 7NW. (See Keswick, Norfolk)
Saddleback Tower	Tower with a gabled roof resembling a saddle.
Septaria	Mud for wall filling as used at Wrabness, Essex.
Sounding board	A board above the lectern for improving the sound.
Spiret	A miniature spire.
Squint (or Hagioscope)	A hole cut through masonry, usually at an oblique angle so that the subsidiary priest could see the High Altar. There is a fine one at Shorehampton, Oxfordshire.
Scratch Dials	(Also known as 'Mass Dials') A sundial, often crudely scratched, on the south wall of a church to indicate the time of Mass, often 9am. There are 30 of these within 10 miles of Cirencester, for example at Ampney Crucis, Ampney St Mary, Coln Rogers, Coln St Dennis, Eastleach Martin, Eastleach Turville, Quenington and Yanworth.
Tie beam roof	A roof with timbers crossing horizontally from one side of the base of the roof to the other and connecting the feet of rafters.
Tympanum	Space enclosed between a lintel and the arch above. Often elaborately carved and over the south door. (See Barfreston, Kent)
Verger	Originally officially responsible for carrying the 'verge' or mace. Nowadays the person responsible for the interior fabric of the church. The sign on some roads 'Danger Soft Verges' does not mean large fat vergers or one that can easily be persuaded!
Vestry	A room attached to a church, possibly once a sacristy where the vestments are kept. It often houses the plate and church registers and is where the clergy prepares for the service.
Wagon Roof	A curved interior roof that looks like the inside of a wagon. For more details on roofs, see Friar, *A Companion to the English Parish Church* (Sutton, 1996), which I have used widely in this glossary.
Wareen	The right to trap rabbits.

BIBLIOGRAPHY

General

Betjeman, J., *Collins Guide to English Parish Churches* (London, 1958)
Bowers, R.F., *In Search of England's Smallest Church* (Workington, 1977)
Cox & Ford, *Parish Churches of England* London (3rd edn) (1941)
Friar, S.A., *Companion Guide to the English Parish Church* (Stroud, 1996)
Jenkins, S., *England's Thousand Best Churches* (London, 1999)
Jones, A.A., *A Thousand Years of the English Parish* (Moreton-in-Marsh, 2000)
Pevsner, *County Guides*
Smith, Cook, Hutton, *English Parish Churches* (London, 1977)
Taylor, A. Clifton, *English Parish Churches as Works of Art* (London, 1974)

County Guides

Cambridgeshire
   Wright, C., *Exploring Cambridgeshire Churches* (Stamford, 1991)
Cheshire
   Salter, M., *The Old Parish Churches of Cheshire* (Malvern, 1995)
Cornwall
   Brown, H.M., *What to Look for in Cornish Churches* (Newton Abbott, 1973)
   Henderson, C., *The Cornish Church Guide* (Truro, reprinted 1964)
Devon
   Hoskins, W.G., *Devon* (London, 3rd edn, 1959)
Dorset
   DHCT, *Dorset Churches* (Dorchester, 1988)
Essex
   Fitch, Canon J., *Essex Churches & Chapels* (Stamford, 1998)
Gloucestershire
   Daubeny, U., *Ancient Cotswold Churches* (London, 1921)
   Lees, H., *Porch and Pew* (Dursley, 1998)
   Verey, D., *Cotswold Churches* (London, 1976)
Herefordshire
   Leonard, J., *Churches of Herefordshire & Their Treasures* (Almeley, 2000)
Isle of Man
   Gelling, Canon J., *A History of the Manx Church 1698-1911* (Manx Heritage Foundation, 1998) *(Very informative, especially on the subject of influential individuals)*
Isle of Wight
   Vivian, V., *Pastoral Pilgrimage* (Freshwater, 1994)
Kent
   Taylor, M., *The Cradle of English Christianity* (Canterbury, 1991)
   Vigar, J., *Kent Churches* (Stroud, 1995)
   Publications of the Romney Marsh HCT
Lincolnshire
   Thorold, H., *Lincolnshire Churches Revisited* (Norwich, 1993)

London
    Leonard, J., *London's Parish Churches* (Derby, 1997)
    Llewellyn, Revd J.F.M., *The Chapels in the Tower of London* (London, 1987)
Norfolk
    Mortlock, D.P. & Roberts, C.V., *The Guide to Norfolk Churches* (Lutterworth Press, 2007)
    Goode, W.J., *Round Tower Churches of S E England* (Burnham Market, 1994) *(Includes Suffolk and Essex)*
Northumberland
    Briggs, G.W.D., *The Medieval Churches of Northumberland* (Newcastle, 2002)
Oxfordshire
    Lethbridge, R., *Oxfordshire Churches* (Witney, 2000)
    Wheeler, R., *Oxfordshire's Best Churches* (Fircone Books Ltd, 2013)
Rutland
    Prophet, J. & Traylen, A.R., *Churches of Rutland* (Stamford, 1988)
Sussex
    Vigar, J., *Exploring Sussex Churches* (Gillingham, 1986)
Wiltshire
    Woodruff, B.J., *Parish Churches of Wiltshire*
Worcestershire
    Bridges, T., *Churches of Worcestershire* (Almeley, 2000)

APPENDIX I

The Churches Conservation Trust
President: HRH the Prince of Wales
8 All Saints Street, London, N1 9RL
0845 303 2760
www.churches.org.uk

The Churches Conservation Trust cares for and promotes public access to over 320 English churches of historic, architectural or archaeological importance which are no longer needed for regular worship. The Trust warmly welcomes visitors – many churches are opened regularly whilst others have key-holders nearby. See the website at www.visitchurches.org.uk for details about each church and information about the Trust, its work and publications.

The Trust now runs coach trips to its churches during the summer together with regular newsletters. To become a supporter contact the Donor Development Assistant on 0800 206 0463 (supporters@thecct.org.uk).

APPENDIX II

Ancient Monuments Society and Friends of Friendless Churches
St Ann's Vestry, 2 Church Entry
London , EC4V 5HB
Tel: 020 72363934
office@friendsoffriendlesschurches.org.uk

AMS was founded in 1924 to conserve and study ancient monuments in Britain, historic buildings and 'fine old craftsmanship'. In 1980 it acquired St Leonards, Spernall, Warwickshire (a small church) and since 1993 has been working in partnership with the Friends of Friendless Churches, an organisation much loved by Sir John Betjeman. Today the Friends own or lease the following churches in England:

Allington Church, Salisbury, Wiltshire
Ayshford Church, Burlescombe, Devon
Ballidon All Saints, Derbyshire
Boveney St Mary Magdalene, near Eton, Buckinghamshire
Brownshill St Mary of the Angels, Gloucestershire

Caldecote St Mary, near Baldock, Hertfordshire
Eastwell St Mary, Ashford, Kent (Ancient Monument with memorial to Richard Plantagenet in churchyard)
Fordham St Mary, Norfolk
Hardmead, Assumption of the Blessed Virgin Mary, Buckinghamshire (has Catesby monument)
Lightcliffe, Old St Matthew, Halifax, Yorkshire (Tower only)
Little Oakley, Corby, Northants
Llancillo, St Peter (recently taken over)
Long Crichel St Mary, Dorset
Matlock, Chapel of St John the Baptist, Derbyshire
Milland, Old St Luke, near Liphook, Sussex (with box pews)
Mundon St Mary, Essex
Papworth St Agnes St John, Nr Huntingdon, Cambridgeshire
Saltfleetby Old St Peter, Louth, Lincolnshire (Tower only)
South Huish St Andrew, Kingsbridge, Devon (ruined nave chancel and tower)
Spernall, St Leonards, Warwickshire
Sutterby St John the Baptist, Lincolnshire
Thornton le Beans, Yorkshire
Urishay, Peterchurch, Herefordshire (former castle chapel, mostly a ruin)
Waddesdon Hill Baptist Chapel, Buckinghamshire
Wickham Bishops St Peter, Essex
Wood Walton, St Andrew, Huntingdon

There are also 20 churches in Wales. For keyholders please contact the office.

APPENDIX III

ASSOCIATIONS

Lincolnshire Old Churches Trust

The Trust was established in 1952 by Lord Ancaster to aid churches that were needing finance to keep them 'wind and watertight'. For many years Henry Thorold was chairman and rescued Brauncewell, Oxcombe and Great Humby (see p.82) These three had become redundant. Humby has now been passed on to a local committee who hold regular services and Oxcombe has been put in the care of the Diocesan Redundant Churches Committee.

The Trust remains in good heart and, with the help of block grants from Waste Recycling Ltd through WREN, it had in the three years up to December 2007 awarded grants of £449,400. The total awarded since 1952 in today's money is fast approaching £1.5 million. The Trust publishes an occasional newsletter and a detailed Annual Report. It can be contacted at PO Box 195, Lincoln LN6 9XR.

National Churches Trust

Our People:
Patron: Her Majesty The Queen
Vice Patron: HRH The Duke of Gloucester KG GCVO ARIBA
Presidents: The Archbishop of Canterbury and The Archbishop of York
To see the full lists of our Vice Presidents, Trustees and Grants Committee: http://www.nationalchurchestrust.org/our-people/our-patron-vice-patron-presidents-and-vice-presidents

Our Grant Schemes:
The National Churches Trust supports a wide variety of projects through its grant programmes. From repairing a roof to helping to install an accessible toilet, its grants help people to continue to serve, and to serve better, their local communities.

Repair Grants: The National Churches Trust's Repair Grants programme offers grants of £10,000 and above towards the cost of urgent and essential structural repair projects. A small number of grants are available at £40,000 and above. Projects must have an estimated cost of at least £100,000 (incl. VAT & fees) to qualify. Places of worship of any denomination and age can apply. We will consider applications from listed and unlisted Christian places of worship across the UK. Other eligibility criteria apply. Decisions on all grant applications are made internally. A shortlist of candidates is discussed twice a year by an independent Grants Committee comprised of experts from the church and heritage sectors.

Community Grants: The National Churches Trust's Community Grants programme offers the opportunity to apply for grants of £5,000 and above for projects which introduce facilities to enable increased community use of places of worship. We are interested in a wide range of projects but all will include toilets and catering facilities. To qualify, projects must have an estimated cost of at least £25,000 (incl. VAT & fees). Other eligibility criteria apply. Decisions on all grant applications are made internally. A shortlist of candidates is discussed by an independent Grants Committee comprised of experts from the church and heritage sectors.

Partnership Grants: The National Churches Trust works with a number of local churches trusts around the UK to offer further help to places of worship. By using their local knowledge and expertise we target grants of £2,500 to £10,000 for urgent repair projects with estimated costs of between £10,000 and £100,000 (including VAT and fees). Applications should be made to your local churches trust, under their usual grant application procedure. They will then decide which projects to put forward under the scheme. Applications for a Partnership Grant cannot be made directly to the National Churches Trust. To find out which local churches trusts are taking part in out Partnership Grant scheme, visit http://www.nationalchurchestrust.org/our-grants/partnership-grants

WREN Grants: Waste Recycling Environmental (WREN) Ltd provides valuable funding for environmental, community and heritage projects. The money comes from the Landfill Communities Fund (LCF) from FCC Environment (previously known as the Waste Recycling Group Ltd). The LCF enables landfill site operators to divert a proportion of their annual landfill tax liability to Environmental Bodies, in this case, WREN. The National Churches Trust is one of WREN's key partners in identifying candidates. We recommend projects at eligible Christian places of worship in England. The fund offers a limited number of grants between £15,000 and £75,000 for urgent structural repair projects supported by other public grant offers and with a minimum cost of £50,000 (including VAT and fees). The programme applies to Grade I or II★ listed buildings sited within 10 miles of a licensed and active landfill site, in a county where FCC Environment currently operates or counties where they used to operate.

Last Year's Grants:
June 2014: £330,000 of funding to 21 churches, chapels and meeting houses. For the full list, including small biographies, visit: http://www.nationalchurchestrust.org/news/latest-grants-safeguard-historic-churches
December 2014: £550,000 of funding to 30 churches, chapels and meeting houses. For the full list, including small biographies, visit: http://www.nationalchurchestrust.org/news/christmas-repair-funding-boost-churches
NB one of our grantee churches in this round was St Mary's in Alton Barnes, Wiltshire, which is considered one of the smallest churches in England. We awarded it a £20,000 National Churches Trust Repair Grant to help fund a major restoration project including repairs to the roof and dealing with damp in the walls and timberwork. (See page 135)

Contact: Georgina Rogerson, Events and Communications Officer
NCT, 31 Newbury Street, London, EC1A 7HV

The Romney Marsh Historic Churches Trust

A letter to *The Times* in 1981 signed by the late Lord Runcie MC, DD, then Archbishop of Canterbury, Mr Richard Ingrams and the late Mr John Piper CH, artist, first drew national attention to the problem of maintaining the medieval churches on Romney Marsh. It prompted an immediate response and the Trust was inaugurated at Leeds Castle on 15 May 1982, with many eminent supporters such as Malcolm Muggeridge, Bishop Ross Hook and HRH Princess Margaret of Hesse.

The Trust's aims are to preserve and maintain the fabric of the 14 medieval churches of Brenzett, Brookland, Burmarsh, Dymchurch, East Guldeford, Fairfield, Ivychurch, Lydd, Newchurch, New Romney, Old Romney, Snargate, Snave and St Mary in the Marsh, together with the three ruined churches of Hope, Midley and Eastbridge. In this book I have included Fairfield (Kent), East Guldeford (East Sussex) and Old Romney (Kent) though the latter is now too large to come into the small category. Unfortunately, Bonnington (Kent) is just the wrong side of the canal to be in the Marsh Trust, but it is nevertheless a small church well worth a visit. Since its foundation, the Trust has awarded grants worth well over £750,000 to the churches and has mounted appeals for special cases such as repair of damage from the great storm of 1987. As well as providing financial help, the Trust offers practical assistance and advice to Parochial Church Councils. One church, St Augustine, Snave, is no longer in regular use and is wholly maintained by the Trust which holds a harvest festival service there each year.

The Trust's Annual General Meeting is held in a different church each year with a guest speaker. Recent speakers include Adam Nicolson, Frank Field MP, Rt. Revd Richard Chartres Bishop of London, and Ptolemy Dean architect to Westminster Abbey. Tours of the churches are arranged for members, and visiting groups are also introduced to the area and its churches on day visits with lunch at one of the local pubs and tea laid on by the WI. Publications include a fully illustrated guide book to the churches, postcards of John Piper's paintings of the churches and Christmas cards from original paintings. The Trust's Annual Report, circulated to all members, gives key arrangements for the churches, some of which have to be kept locked.

Substantial funds are still required to maintain and preserve these beautiful churches both for current and future generations. We urge you to join the Trust and help in its work to secure the future of these beautiful and unique churches.

Further information can be obtained from the Hon. Secretary, Mrs Elizabeth Marshall, Lansdell House, Rolvenden, Kent TN17 4LW, email sec@romneychurches.net.

The Round Tower Churches Society

There are 175 churches with round towers still standing in England, mostly situated in East Anglia, and a few more towers surviving in a ruinous state. Many date back to early times, with a few being built in Saxon and Norman times, and with some of the towers being updated with later octagonal belfries or built new till about 1400 AD, and then a few Victorian ones.

This Society exists to raise awareness of these precious ancient buildings, to give help and advice, and to support their congregations with grants for restoration work. There are regular church tours arranged each summer to encourage people to visit these churches and to learn more about them. The annual subscription provides four magazines a year, with articles of interest to the members and reports on recent research and developments.

Round Tower Churches Society
Crabbe Hall, Burnham Market
King's Lynn, PE31 8EN

Further details are available on the website www.roundtowers.org.uk or on Facebook or Twitter.

INDEX OF CHURCHES BY PLACE NAME

Acton Burnell, Langley Chapel 108
Alton Barnes, St Mary 135
Alton Priors, All Saints 135
Apley, St Andrew 83
Arne, St Nicholas 43
Aston-sub-Edge, St Andrew 54
Avington, St Mark and St Luke 15
Babingley Chapel 92
Baddesley Clinton, St Michael 129
Ballaugh, Old Kirk 68
Barfreston, St Nicholas 72
Bassenthwaite, St Bega 32, 33
Bedmond, Church of the Ascension 62
Betteshanger, St Mary 74
Billesley, All Saints 128
Billington, St Michael and All Angels 12
Bittering Parva, St Peter 92
Blackland, St Peter 134
Boarhunt, St Nicholas 56
Bodinnick, St John the Baptist 31
Bonchurch, St Boniface 70
Bonnington, St Rumwold 73
Boveney, St Mary Magdalene 20
Bradford-on-Avon:
    St Mary 134
    St Laurence 132, 133
Bradwell-Juxta-Mare, St Peter-on-the-Wall 48
Brentor, St Michael de Rupe 36
Bredwardine, St Andrew 61
Brookland, St Augustine 73
Buntingford, St Peter 64
Burton Lazars, St James 80
Buttermere, St James 132
Byrness, St Francis of Assisi 96
Cambridge:
    Fitzwilliam College Chapel 22, 23
    St Mary Magdalene 23
    St Peter 22
Carburton, St Giles 99
Chapel-le-Dale, St Leonard 144
Childwickbury, St Mary 62
Chiselhampton, St Katherine 102
Cold Weston, St Mary 109
Compton:
    Watts Chapel 121
    St Nicholas 122
Cowley, St Laurence 89, 90
Cregneash, St Peter 68
Culbone, St Beuno 110, 111
Dalby, St James 67

Dale Abbey, All Saints 34
Dalwood, Loughwood Meeting House 39
Deerhurst, Odda's Chapel 54
Derby, Bridge Chapel 35
Didling, St Andrew 126
Downside, St Michael's Chapel 121
Drayton, St James 78
Duntisbourne Rous, St Michael 50
East Guldeford, St Mary 73, 124
East Marden, St Peter 126
East Shefford, St Thomas 15
Edworth, St George 13
Elkstone, St John 51
Elsted, St Paul 127
Elstone Chapel 100
Escomb, St John the Evangelist 45
Esher, St George 120
Exeter:
    St Pancras 37
    St Petrock 37
    St Stephen 36
Fairfield, St Thomas a Becket 73
Far Sawrey, St Peter 77
Farmcote, St Faith 53
Farndish, St Michael 11
Fifield Bavant, St Martin 131
Fleet Marston, St Mary 18
Ford, St Andrew 127
Fordon, St James 138
Fourstones, St Aidan 97
Framland Churches 80
Frenze, St Andrew 92
Furtho, St Bartholomew 95
Gibside Chapel 46
Goltho, St George 82
Great Humby Chapel 82
Guernsey, St Apolline 25
Guyhirn Chapel 24
Hales, St Margaret 93
Hanley Childe, St Michael 136
Hannah, St Andrew 83
Haydon (Old Church), St Cuthbert 97
Heath Chapel 107
Heysham:
    St Patrick's Chapel 76
    St Peter 76
Honeychurch, St Mary 38
Hoveton, St Peter 91
Idsworth, St Hubert 58
Iffley, St Mary the Virgin 104

INDEX OF CHURCHES BY PLACE NAME

Inkpen, St Michael 15
Ireby, Old Church 33
Isle of Wight, St Lawrence Old Church 69
Jersey, The Fishermen's Chapel, 19
Jordans, Friends Meeting House 20
Keele University Chapel 115
Kelloe, St Helen 46
Keswick, All Saints 92
Kilpeck, St Mary and St David 61
Lathom, St James 76
Lead, St Mary 144
Leigh, All Saints 135
Little Gidding, St John 65
Little Hormead, St Mary 64
Little Kimble, All Saints 17
Little Stanmore, St Lawrence 90
Little Washbourne, St Mary 53
Littleborough, St Nicholas 100
Llancillo, St Peter 60
Llandough, St Dochwy 27
London:
    St Ethelburga 88
    St Olave 87
    St Pancras 88
    Tower of 84-6
Loughwood Meeting House 39
Lower Sapey, St Bartholomew 137
Lullington, Good Shepherd 123
Malew, St Mark 68
March, St Wendreda 24
Marden Churches 125, 126
Marton-in-the-Forest, St Mary 141
Melverley, St Peter 108
Mepal, St Mary 21
Midhopestones, St James 143
Nately Scures, St Swithin 57
Nether Worton, St James 102
North Marden, St Mary 125
Northwood, Mt Vernon Hospital Chapel 90
Oborne, St Cuthbert 41
Old Bewick, Holy Trinity 47
Old Romney, St Clement 73
Outhgill, St Mary 130
Paddlesworth, St Benedict 72
Paddlesworth, St Oswald 74
Plumpton, St John the Baptist 94
Potsgrove, St Mary 13
Radwell, All Saints 63
Romney Marsh, St Mary-in-the Marsh 73
Rycote, St Michael 104
Saltersford, Jenkin Chapel 28
Setchey, St Mary 93
Shefford Woodlands, St Stephen 14

Shelland, King Charles the Martyr 116
Shelsley Walsh, St Andrew 137
Shelve, All Saints 109
Shobdon, St John the Evangelist 61
Shocklach, St Edith 27
Shorthampton, All Saints 103
Sisland, St Mary 93
Slitting Mill, St John the Baptist 114
Sookholme, St Augustine 100
South Elmham, All Saints 119
Speeton, St Leonard 139
St Margarets, St Margaret 61
Steeple, St Lawrence 48
Steventon, St Nicholas 59
Stidd, St Saviour 75
Stockwood, St Edwold 40
Sutton Bassett, St Mary 95
Sutton Bingham, All Saints 113
Sutton Cheney, St James 78, 79
Swell, St Catherine, 112
Syde, St Mary 51
Tattenhoe, St Giles 19
Temple, St Catherine 31
Theydon Mount, St Michael 49
Thockrington, St Aidan 97
Thorington, St Peter 119
Thornham Parva, St Mary 117
Tickencote, St Peter and St Paul 106
Tixover, St Mary Magdalene 106
Trentishoe, St Peter 39
Trevalga, St Petrock 29
Tushingham, Old St Chad 28
Up Marden, St Michael 126
Waddingworth, St Margaret 82
Warburton, St Werburgh 28
Wardley, St Botolph 105
Wareham, St Martin 44
Wasdale Head, St Olaf 33
Waterden, All Saints 93
Watford, Oxhey Chapel 64
Weeke, St Matthew 59
Well, St Margaret 83
Wendens Ambo, St Mary the Virgin 49
Whitwell, St Mary and St Rhadegunde 70
Widemouth Bay, Our Lady and St Anne 30
Widford, St Oswald 103
Willen, St Mary Magdalene 19
Winterborne Tomson, St Andrew 41
Withersdale, St Mary Magdalene 119
Worth Matravers, St Aldheim 42
Wrabness, All Saints 47
Yelford, St Nicholas and St Swithun 101

GENERAL INDEX

Aelfric 55
Aidan 48
Aldermans 11
Aldhelm 133
Alexandria 92
Allington, Revd J. 106
Alveston 128
Armitage, Lydall 92
Art Nouveau 90, 121, 144
Astor, Baron 94
Austen family 59, 72

Babbington-Smith family 101
Bateman, J. 83
Bates, T. 105
Becket, Thomas a 73
Bell, J. 109
Benn, Flt. Lt. 48
Bertha, Queen 71
Beuno, St 110, 111
Beveridge, Lord 97
Braesnose College 116
Breamore 52
Burnt Norton 54
Burrowbridge 37, 102
Busby 19

Calf of Man 68
Canada 30, 57
Carleton, General 57
Carleton, Guy 57
Caröe 73
Catcleugh Resevoir 97
Catesby 79
Chancellor, F. 48
Charles I, King 38, 65, 104, 116
Charles II, King 9, 91
Charlestown 71
Chatsworth 34
Chitty Chitty Bang Bang 80
Civil War 123
Claremont 120
Clifford, Lady Anne 130
Columba, St 88
Commonwealth 139
Cromwell 11, 24, 65, 123
Cymbeline's Mount 17

DeGleyn 49
Derby, Earl of 76

Disney, Walt 70
Dodd, William 90
Dudley, Lord Guildford 85
Dutems, Revd 96
Dymoke, Edward 82

Ebbsfleet 71
Eddowes, Robert 57
Eden, Sir Anthony 131
Edward I, King 86
Edward the Confessor 55
Edward the Martyr 133
Eliot, T.S. 54, 65, 66
Eloi, St 103
Ely Cathedral 21
Ermin Street 50
Essex, Earl of 85
Ethelbert, King 71
Ethelred, King 133

Ferrar, Nicholas 65
Fettiplace family 15
Four Quartets 65

Galtres, Forest of 141
Gee, George 76
George III, King 27
Ghazi I, King 44
Gibbons, Grinling 90
Gill, Eric 104
Glanfield, E.B. 87
Glorious, HMS 30
Grey, Henry 85
Grey, Lady Jane 80, 85
Griggs, F. 126
Gunpowder Plot 9

Haddon Hall 34
Hagley Hall 115
Hall, Marshall 135
Hann, Revd Isaac 39
Hardy, Thomas 41
Hardwick Hall 34
Harrison Sutton 37
Hathaway, Anne 128
Hatter, Mad 34
Hayle Abbey 94
Henniker-Major, Lady 118
Henry III, King 84
Henry VII, King 85, 124

GENERAL INDEX

Henry VIII, King 54
Hobnails Inn 53
Hooke, Robert 19
Hoskins, W.G. 38
Howard, Thomas 85
Hungerford 14
Hwicce 54

Jacobites 108
Jane Eyre 106
Jenner 42
Jesty, B. 42
Jesus College, Oxford 94
Jones, Canon 132

Kelly, Fleur 58
Kempe 134
Kennington, Eric 44
Kettles Yard 23
Kilvert 61
Kingdon brothers 30
Knottesford, Revd 128

Lake District 75
Landmark Trust 80
Lansdowne, Lord 135
Lawrence of Arabia 44
Lee, W.A. 65
Leigh-Hunt, Revd 132
Lepers 24
Lynton 39

Maastricht, Bishop of 58
MacCormack, Sir R. 22
Mack, Revd 91
Malmesbury 133
Manchester Ship Canal 28
Mark, King of Cornwall 18
Marlborough 30
Marston Moor 99
Mary of Modena, Queen 21
Mazine, John 99
More, Sir Thomas 86
Mustard Pot Inn 143

Nairn, Ian 126
National Trust 39
Navasota, RMS 37
Nesbit, E. 73
Newcastle, Duke of 120, 37
Nicholson 106
Nott, Bishop 92
Nottingham, Duke of 99

Olaf, St 33
Old Bolingbroke 81
Old Ferry Inn 31
Orthona 48
Oswald, St 103
Overbury, Sir Thomas 85

Patrick, St 76
Peers, Sir C.P. 102
Pelham, Hon. C.A. 69
Pepys 87
Platt, Richard 88
Platt, William 88
Poppins, Mary 58
Potter, Beatrix 77, 117
Pre-Raphaelites 70
Purbeck, Isle of 40

Quakers 20
Quatremaine family 104

Rame Head 29
Ratcliffe 79
Regina, HMS 30
Ribblehead Viaduct 145
Ribchester 75
Richard II, King 25
Richard III, King 26, 141, 142
Robin Hood 99
Rockingham Castle 78
Rolfe, C.C. 16
Rouse, E. Clive 18
Royal Military Canal 73

Sampford Courtenay 38
Sarratt 62
Scheemakers 74
Scott, Captain 33
Scott, Sir G. Gilbert 70
Shakespeare 128
Shelshall Priory 18
Shore, Col. 38
Smiley 62
Spence, Basil 118
Stanhope, Earl 35
Stanley, Lady 76
Stephens, B. 30
Stiperstones 109
St Augustine of Canterbury 71
St Helena 46
Swinbrook 103
Swinburne, A.C. 70

Tennyson 33, 70
Terri the dog 55
Thorold, Henry 61, 82
Tom Jones 82
Tratt, John 38
Trevose Head 30

Uppingham 105

Van der Post, Ingaret 37
Victoria, Queen 108
Voysey, C.F. 90, 111

Wasdale Head Hotel 33
Webb, Kirsten 43

Welch, John 67
Wendreda, St 24
Wesley, J. 19
Westmacott 102
Westminster Abbey 102
Wingfield-Digby family 155
William III, King 28
Worcester, Bishop of 103
Woburn 13
Wolfe, General 57
World War I 12, 14, 102
World War II 48, 98, 102

Zborowski, Counts 80

Also by John Kinross

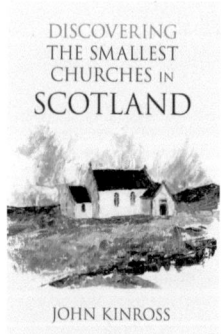

Discovering the Smallest Churches in Scotland

£12.99

ISBN 978 0 7524 5880 9

www.thehistorypress.co.uk

Discovering the Smallest Churches in Wales

£13.99

ISBN 978 0 7524 4101 6

www.thehistorypress.co.uk